The President's Pianist

The President's Pianist

◆

My Term with Truman
and My Life in Music

George Manos,
as told to Daniel Lindley

iUniverse, Inc.
New York Bloomington Shanghai

The President's Pianist
My Term with Truman and My Life in Music

iUniverse books may be ordered through booksellers or by contacting:

iUniverse
1663 Liberty Drive
Bloomington, IN 47403
www.iuniverse.com
1-800-Authors (1-800-288-4677)

Because of the dynamic nature of the Internet, any Web addresses or links contained in this book may have changed since publication and may no longer be valid.

The views expressed in this work are solely those of the author and do not necessarily reflect the views of the publisher, and the publisher hereby disclaims any responsibility for them.

ISBN: 978-0-595-48716-5 (pbk)
ISBN: 978-0-595-49127-8 (cloth)
ISBN: 978-0-595-60812-6 (ebk)

Printed in the United States of America

To Nick and Helen Santrizos

Contents

Introduction

I've spent seven decades in music. During my career as a concert pianist and symphony conductor, I've worked with some of the great musicians of the 20th century, including singers like Todd Duncan and Elena Nikolaidi, and composers and conductors like Aaron Copland, Leonard Bernstein, and Leopold Stokowski. As a young piano student, I even attended classes taught by a woman who had known Brahms when she was a girl in Germany.

My most famous musical acquaintance came early in my career, and he was better known in another line of work. I first met President Harry S. Truman when I was nearly 20 years old and still studying the intricacies of piano, voice, and conducting at the Peabody Conservatory of Music in Baltimore. Truman was a professional politician, rather than a professional musician. Unlike many in politics today, he wasn't afraid to call himself a politician. In fact, he considered the best professional politicians more honest and more important to the commonweal than the big businessmen and bankers of his day.

Truman was also an amateur musician. Thus came my years, when I was a young man, as his personal piano player. He loved classical piano music, and I was picked to play for him. I became his White House pianist, as the position was called, in the summer before he was elected to his second term in office. I was known as the White House pianist even though I never actually played in the White House, which was being renovated for much of Truman's second term as president. He lived and worked for most of that time nearby, at the Blair-Lee House.

We Americans don't often associate music with politics. But Truman's interest in music shouldn't be surprising. He was a concert pianist manqué. As a boy in Missouri, he'd studied and played piano for years. Throughout his adult life, from his years as a soldier and then a haberdasher to his long, successful career as a politician, he continued to play, though just for fun. A straightforward and direct man, Truman seemed to love music for the truths it spoke to him—truths of emotion, scale, and proportion.

In 1948, as a young member of the Marine Band, I became Truman's personal pianist, a position that I continued in through his second term in office. In those years, I developed a profound respect for the man. Not just for his musical taste, which was high. But also for his character. He had a sense of decency rare in any age, especially in our own troubled times. Despite the pressures of the world that weighed on him while he was president, he always treated me and those around him courteously and well. In fact, he acted toward me as a good father does to his son.

Several years ago, I went to Constitution Hall in Washington, D.C., a place where I'd often performed during a long and fruitful musical career and where Truman had frequently attended concerts during his years in Washington. I made the short trip that night from my home in Bethesda to that huge performance hall to meet David McCullough, the historian who wrote the best biography of Truman and who was giving a lecture. After his talk, McCullough and I chatted. The author said he was sorry he hadn't known of my relationship with the president while he was researching *Truman*.

A few years later, when I was at the Harry S. Truman Presidential Library and Museum in Missouri to celebrate an anniversary, Kathy Knotts, a vice president at the museum at the time, told me that I was one of the few people still alive who had worked with Truman. I was one of the last who'd known the man and still had first-hand insights into the actions and character of this historic figure.

So, in the interest of filling in those small blank spots of history, in the following pages I've set down my memories of Truman, perhaps one of the best presidents this country has ever had. He certainly ranks among the most underrated. Along the way, I've recorded the musical milieu of the 20th century that shaped my own career as a pianist and conductor. A century of turmoil and struggle, it was Truman's milieu as well.

1

The Greek-American Children

My entry into the musical realm came early, and on my own initiative.

When I was a child, the Manos family lived in a big house with a wraparound porch. My father, a Greek immigrant, was named Spiros, but everybody called him Frank because they couldn't remember his Greek name. My mother also had come from Greece. Her given name was Marina, but she went by Mary in this new country of America.

I was born on March 10, 1928, the last of my parents' four children, in Greensboro, North Carolina, where I spent most of my early childhood. My family moved to Norfolk, Virginia, for a few years when my father's work took him there, but a little later we moved back to Greensboro.

My three siblings were already studying music by the time I was walking and talking. Although neither of my parents played an instrument, both loved to listen to music. It was said that several ancestors and relatives in Greece had been accomplished musicians. My parents no doubt considered musical instruction an important part of a well-rounded education—a common belief in those days, but one that seems to have fallen by the wayside, alas.

My older sister, Bes, took violin lessons. The next in line, Helen, studied piano under a teacher who came to our house every week. My brother, Andrew, didn't take to music, and managed to talk his way out of lessons. He was far more interested in baseball at the time. Years later, his sporting enthusiasm almost paid off in a big way when he got a chance to try out for the Brooklyn Dodgers at Ebbets Field. He hit and fielded well during tryouts. But he was a big man. He ran slowly and he was no good at sliding. He didn't make the cut. He gave up on fame, but eventually went on to fortune as the founder and owner of a highly successful automobile dealership in Bethesda, Maryland.

When I was just four or five, I became fascinated with the piano lessons that my sister Helen was taking. No one seemed to notice my interest. When Helen practiced with her teacher in the living room, I'd hide behind the piano and listen. Then, after the piano teacher had gone home and when nobody was looking, I'd sit down at the piano and replay the lesson from memory. Sometimes I'd just play at odd hours when no one was around. This went on for a year or so until one day Helen's teacher walked in a bit early, before Helen had returned from school, and heard me playing the previous week's lesson. She said to my mother: "Mrs. Manos, this is the one who should be studying the piano!" And so I began to take lessons and play.

To this day I can remember the first three or four bars of one of the pieces that Helen used to practice with her teacher. It was by John Thompson, the creator of many piano study books, some of which are still in use by students today. That simple song, "By a Roadside Fire," remained for many years the only song that Helen could perform on the piano. Whenever she'd play it, even in adulthood, I'd come to the piano bench after she was through, sit down, and play it again. We'd share a good laugh.

Like my brother, Helen soon discovered that music wasn't her calling. She quit lessons shortly after I started. When she grew up, she went on to a successful career in journalism, working for Eleanor Medill "Cissy" Patterson and the *Washington Times-Herald* in Washington, D.C. Later, she moved to New York City to take a job with the famed fashion publicist Eleanor Lambert—the woman who started New York's Fashion Week.

After a bit of study, I began to enjoy some local success. Early on, I won several prizes for recitals I gave in Norfolk and Greensboro. Word got around. One day a Southern gentleman named Major Ridge approached my parents and asked if it would be OK if my sister and I played weekly radio concerts for his local radio station in Greensboro, WBIG. I'm not exactly sure how Major Ridge heard of me. The first time we met, I was in one of my usual childhood habitats, on the softball field with a bunch of kids playing ball a couple of blocks from home.

Although my sister and I weren't paid for our radio performances, we were delighted with our weekly program. Every Sunday, Bes and I would play for a half hour at three o'clock on the radio show Major Ridge had titled *The Greek-American Children*. As the offspring of Greek immigrants, we were viewed as exotic in the rural South. In fact, we were greatly hated. We were in the bosom of Southern Baptism and Methodism, after all. But we were just kids, for God's sake.

We persevered. Throughout my career, especially during my formative early years, I had the unwavering support and encouragement of my loving parents, my brother, and my sisters. I cannot over-emphasize the vital importance of this genuine and strong family love and support throughout my career in music. It was to me a linchpin.

My sister and I played our radio recitals in the studios of Greensboro's O'Henry Hotel, about six blocks from the ball field. I'd usually be playing softball Sunday afternoons when someone would yell, "It's time to go!" Off I'd run to the O'Henry to assume my role as precocious pianist. For half an hour I'd hammer at the keys while Bes fiddled away with all her heart. We performed serious music: selections from Schubert's *Sonata for Violin and Piano*, for instance. Although we earned no money, we received plenty of praise and recognition in person and in the local press. We loved it. At home, we'd faithfully practice our repertoire together.

One of three announcers would introduce us for each show: Bob Poole; the strangely named Kaski Narve; or Jack Armstrong. I only got to know Armstrong well. He was also the announcer for the Wednesday night fights in Greensboro. He'd let my brother and me in for free every week so that we could watch the professional and amateur matches staged there. Andy and I sat right next to Armstrong ringside as he called the fight blow by blow over the radio, and we loved it.

Inspired by the fights and by our love of sports, we had the bright idea to set up our own boxing arena for kids. Our house, which we liked to call a McKinley Stinker—a big, old Victorian, that is, in the slang of those days—had a spacious porch with sturdy columns. After a trip to a local lumber yard, Andy and I used cardboard and plywood we'd bought to convert the porch into a miniature boxing ring. We'd go in to our makeshift arena and beat the hell out of one other. We charged the local kids two cents' admission to watch.

My father thought this was disgusting—so disgusting that he decided to register his displeasure by making a lasting impression. He was friends with the local police chief and fire chief. So he arranged to have them raid our little enterprise. They came on a rainy night, collared us, and hauled us off downtown. Soon my father appeared and got us out. He took us home, bawled us out, and made us tear down our miniature coliseum. Then he ordered my brother to do his homework and me to practice my piano. Thus did I lurch another step toward a life in music.

Was I a musical prodigy? I don't know. I just did what I was told. My parents said practice. I practiced. They said perform. I performed. In looking back, I much appreciate their true support and perseverance.

Within a few years, I was outgrowing the talents of my piano teacher, and Bes of her violin teacher. So my father moved our family to Washington, D.C. Washington was still a small Southern city in those days, not much bigger than a town, really, but it offered cultural opportunities far beyond those of Greensboro.

It seemed the ideal place for the whole family. My father could find work in Washington, even during the tail end of the Great Depression. First he had a job with the Royal Pilsen Brewing Company. Then he got into the drugstore business. Bes and I would meanwhile benefit from the city's more advanced music scene. We also dreamed of someday perhaps attending the famed Peabody Conservatory of Music, then the best music school in the nation, only a few miles down the road in Baltimore.

Bes and I did eventually enter the Peabody Conservatory and became professional musicians. Years later, Bes established a career as a concert violinist in Rochester, New York, but later gave it up to raise a family. I continued and went on to become President Truman's personal pianist, the prelude to my long and varied career in music.

2

Music Lessons

When we came to Washington in 1939, the Manos family first lived in downtown D.C., not far from where the National Gallery of Art was to be built a few years later. Little did I know then that the National Gallery would become a future employer of mine, and a major part of my life. There were a lot of beautiful houses in that part of town when we lived there, but most of them have since been torn down.

I remember little of the move to Washington other than our father driving the family car on the long ride north from Greensboro. After settling in our new home, our parents soon had all of us children pursuing our education. I started middle school at the Gales School, in a small, historic building near Union Station and New York Avenue. Gradually all of us, except for my brother, Andy, shed our Southern accents.

I followed my brother and sisters later to Jefferson Junior High in Southwest Washington, a neighborhood where black families were pouring in from the South due to growing job opportunities in the nation's capital as World War II ramped up. Jefferson Junior High had a kindly, well-educated principal, Hugh Stewart Smith, who also happened to love music. In fact, he was an excellent pianist. As an educator, he was so well regarded in Washington that members of the U.S. Congress consulted with him before awarding Fulbright scholarships.

As soon as Smith got his hands on me and my sister Bes, he had me playing the piano and Bes fiddling away like mad at school recitals and other events. This continued at McKinley High School, which Bes and I attended after Jefferson. McKinley had its own orchestra, a big one of 75 or 80 pieces. It was among the oldest in the city, and had been the first to play at the D.A.R.'s grand Constitution Hall at 18th and D streets.

The D.A.R. was infamous at the time for not allowing blacks in the cavernous building—not even in a segregated section. The group wouldn't even let the great black singer Marian Anderson perform there when she wanted to give a recital.

That's when Eleanor Roosevelt stepped in. With the power of her husband, President Franklin Delano Roosevelt, behind her, she reserved the first flight of steps up the Lincoln Memorial so that Anderson could give an outdoor concert in the National Mall. Mrs. Roosevelt had a concert grand placed out in the open. On Easter Sunday, 1939, Marian Anderson, with a white accompanist, gave a complete recital on the steps of the Lincoln Memorial. She sang spirituals like "He's Got the Whole World in His Hands." The huge crowd was a sea of appreciative faces, mostly black. There were so many people there that you could barely see the Lincoln Memorial. I witnessed this historic event, and it was thrilling.

Seeing our promise as musicians, Principal Smith found a first-rate music teacher named Daisy Fickensher for us. Miss Fickensher was a full-time music teacher who taught privately in an enormous house she owned on Rock Creek Church Road. Luckily for me and Bes, Miss Fickensher could play piano and violin. So she could teach both of us. Her brother, Arthur Fickensher, was a distinguished composer who lived in California. Daisy Fickensher knew people like Percy Grainger, the pianist and composer who had been born in Australia but who had gained world renown as a player and composer of classical music in England and the United States.

We got some sophisticated training from Miss Fickensher, who must have been in her 60s or 70s, but still had great energy. She was a distinguished woman with a noble bearing. She had a beautiful head of gray hair, which she wore short. She was always elegantly dressed and mannered. She acted like what she was: an aristocrat. A musical aristocrat.

Daisy Fickensher had so many students that she'd started her own string orchestra. On Mondays I'd travel to her house for my piano lessons. On Wednesdays I'd go with my sister Bes and accompany her on piano as Bes worked through her violin lesson. Friday nights Bes and I would return, and I'd play the piano to accompany Miss Fickensher's string orchestra. Her foyer was bigger than most living rooms. Still, she had to scatter her orchestra, which must have numbered 20 or 25. It ranged through the foyer, living room, and dining room. At these rehearsals, Miss Fickensher would play cello while conducting with her bow.

I learned a lot from Miss Fickensher. The most important part of my education with her was very general but very useful: a sound exposure to a wide range of the classics. That helped me enormously during my later studies at the Peabody Conservatory.

All the while, I kept up my studies at McKinley, and then some. The powers-that-be at the high school had discovered my musical talents, and decided to make full use of them. McKinley had a locally made Lewis & Hitchcock organ in its auditorium. Lewis & Hitchcock were well-known organ makers in Washington—a company of high quality, like another nearby and well-known organ manufacturer, the Mohler Organ Company in Frederick, Maryland. I began studying the pipe organ, and then playing it for school events.

When the school administration found out that I played piano too, they put me to work giving piano recitals. I'd give piano and organ recitals almost every week. When it was discovered that I loved to conduct, the administration also got me conducting the school's orchestra. There was a fine men's glee club in town called the Joseph M. Daniels Glee Club, and I began conducting that group too. Plus inter-high school choruses and mixed choruses.

By my second year of high school, I was so weighed down with practice and work that often I wouldn't get home until 10 or 11 at night. My mother or father would ask, "Where have you been?" I'd say, "I've been at school." Often my parents said nothing in reply. But I could tell by the looks on their faces that they thought I'd been catting about town. The longer this continued, the more suspicious they seemed to become.

Finally I had to call Principal Smith, my musical protector and divine interloper, to intercede. He came over to our house and explained my popularity with school officials to my parents. "Well, that's what's happened to George," he said as he wound up his talk. "This kid is so talented they've got him doing everything."

Smith helped ease my parents' minds. And he was speaking truthfully. I was doing everything. But it was becoming too much. Finally, one day, it just came to me. I don't need this, I concluded. I decided to walk out of school. As I headed down the hall toward the door, the assistant principal stopped me and said, "Where do you think you're going?"

"I'm going home."

"Why?"

"I've had enough of this school."

And I had. I walked home, which was a long way, five or six miles. There was no car for me because it was wartime and gasoline was rationed. Even though my father had somehow finagled a B gas card as well as an A card, it still wasn't enough for me to get enough fuel to drive to school. It took a couple of hours for me to walk from the McKinley school in Northeast Washington to the place we'd moved to in Northwest Washington, but at least I'd blown off some steam by the time I got home.

Soon after I'd reached the refuge of the Manos house, however, I heard from the assistant principal who'd intercepted me at the door.

"Come back tomorrow with your mother and father, or else," he warned over the telephone.

I didn't. I was sick of it. So I was expelled.

I didn't care. In fact, I was delighted. I felt as if a huge weight had been lifted from my shoulders. They had simply been putting too much responsibility on a teenage kid.

I seemed to be at a dead end. But not for long. Within a week or two, my old champion, Principal Hugh Stewart Smith, came by. What a wonderful friend this man turned out to be! My parents adored him, and so did the rest of the family. He was a gentleman and an educator, a marvelous man, a treasure to my family and to me.

Principal Smith told us that he'd arranged with Mae Bradshaw, the principal of another school, Roosevelt High, to get me out of my predicament. I'd be required to attend Roosevelt, but only in the mornings. My afternoons would be free so that I could attend the Peabody Conservatory in Baltimore. It was the best music school in the country, after all, and the place where I really wanted to be.

Mae Bradshaw saw to it that I took the basics at Roosevelt High in the morning: English, history, and math, among other things. My afternoons I'd devote to the Peabody Conservatory, some 35 miles away in Baltimore—if I could get in, of course.

To find out, I traveled by train to the Peabody as soon as possible. When I got there, I was auditioned by Reginald Stewart, director of the Conservatory and conductor of the Baltimore Symphony Orchestra. Although barely in his 40s, Stewart had already enjoyed a long and distinguished career in the United States, Canada, and England, in addition to Baltimore. He'd led orchestras in New York, Washington, and Detroit, and founded the Toronto Bach Choir.

I finished playing, and I passed muster with Stewart. I must have looked very happy as I got up to head for the door.

"Wait a minute," Stewart said. "You have to be auditioned by the piano teacher. Who do you want to study with?"

"Austin Conradi," I said. I had tremendous respect for Conradi, who I knew taught at the Peabody. He wasn't physically impressive. In fact, he was a small man. But then, so was the biblical David. Conradi had fingers made of steel. He'd been raised in a musical family in Baltimore, and was a master of the piano. He could convey almost any emotion with the instrument, from rapturous romanticism to steely resolve.

I went to Conradi's studio full of trepidation. The master turned out to be serious but not intimidating. He wasn't mean at all. In fact, he was very nice. By the tone of his voice, he seemed very imposing, and I was shaking at the outset. But he saw that I was young, and he was gentle with me. The only way he could tell if I was worth taking on as a student, however, was to sit me down in front of a Steinway and have me play. He put me on the piano bench and said, "First, I want you to play something slow. Then I want you to play something fast. Then I want you to play something that's full of virtuoso elements."

So I played. I didn't know it then, but he later told me that he'd just wanted to see how I controlled sound. I must have passed the test. I ran through the scales, played slow and then fast. Finally, I played something "highly technical," in his words. I think I chose an etude by the Russian composer Anton Rubenstein for my first audition.

Anyway, I got through it.

"OK," he said with a shrug. "We'll take you on."

I was elated. I'd finally found a place where I could really learn. At McKinley High, I'd had plenty of practice—too much, in fact—but no mentorship. Daisy Fickensher, my private music instructor, was a wonderful teacher, but her interest lay as much in strings as in the piano. She'd taken me as far down the road as we could go.

"How do you do it?" Conradi asked me the day of my audition at the Peabody.

"I don't know," I said.

And that was true. My musical talent was something that was just there. It was a natural thing, something I'd been born with.

Conradi said: "OK. Now we're going to teach you how to do it properly so you can think about it."

And boy, was that torture. The first year with my new mentor, the position of every finger had to be analyzed and judged just right. I had the technique, but I didn't know what I was doing, until Conradi taught me how to do it. To this day, if I try to play music that I knew before I studied with him, I can't do it. Because it was instinct. Pure instinct. Professional piano playing required the discipline of understanding and practice that Conradi taught.

Things began to click. In the mornings, I'd attend Roosevelt High to get my basic academic requirements out of the way. Then I'd ride the streetcar, for a dime, to Washington's Union Station, where I'd catch the train to Baltimore. The fare, for some reason, was $1.01. Not one dollar, but $1.01.

Then I hit another bureaucratic snag. I had to have a high-school degree to continue to study at the Peabody, the administration there had decided. Once more the resourceful Hugh Stewart Smith stepped into the breach. He discovered that by taking and passing an advanced exam in a foreign language, I could get the credit that I needed for my high-school degree.

I'd grown up speaking and writing Greek, so a test in modern Greek seemed like a slam dunk. Columbia University offered such an exam, which could be administered in my hometown of Washington.

Principal Smith arranged for me to take the test at the Franklin School, headquarters for the city's public schools. On the day of the test, I was taken into a big room, where I was the only student, and given lots of papers. These would be self-explanatory, my testers told me. Half the papers were in English, and half were in Greek. I had to translate. I had to conjugate verbs. I had to run through the declensions of nouns. I studied before the test, of course, but I was glad that I'd grown up bilingual. In fact, as the baby of the family, I'd seldom spoken English when I was a boy at home in the South. I hadn't even entered school until the third or fourth grade. My brother taught me some American phrases and I also learned English from friends and on the softball field.

The hardest part of the Greek test at the Franklin School came when I had to translate a couple of paragraphs of a speech by President Franklin D. Roosevelt into Greek. I did the best I could. I had a little difficulty with the Greek script. I couldn't always remember where accents were supposed to go. I decided to put the accent over the syllable that should be properly accented in speech. But there were other syllables that seemed to cry for accents. Years later I discussed the question with an old Greek teacher of mine. "Well," he said, "you probably did all right. There are no rules."

"Now you tell me!" I said.

The funny thing is that the Greek Parliament later passed a law wiping out all those extraneous accents, except for the ones where the word is supposed to be accented when speaking. It's just a little slash. Today, when I read anything printed in Greek, I seldom even see accents. The Greeks got wise. They turned around and destroyed all the accents. Just rubbed them out. You could almost hear a national, collective sigh of relief.

Now that I had my high-school diploma in hand, my future at the Peabody Conservatory seemed secure. My sister Bes had auditioned at the Peabody too, with the great violinist Oscar Shumsky, likened to the even greater Heifetz by some. She too had outgrown the wonderful Daisy Fickensher. Bes, who'd already graduated from high school, also was duly accepted. Sometimes we'd ride the train to the Peabody together. Her career as a professional musician ended years later only because she decided to start a family.

Meanwhile, I was benefiting from my cultural immersion in Washington. I got to meet people like Hans Kindler, the music director of the National Symphony, which performed at Constitution Hall. In those days, I'd simply walk backstage after a concert, introduce myself to Kindler, and talk, even though I was just a kid. Now it would be difficult even to reach a man in his position on the telephone.

Kindler, a Dutchman whose full name was Johannes Hendrikus Kindler, was a cellist and conductor who'd founded the National Symphony Orchestra in 1931, and remained its leader up until his death in 1949. He was very kind to me. Years later I served as president of the Hans Kindler Foundation, which was set up to fund new chamber music and underwrite performances in his memory.

The program at the Peabody Conservatory was rigorous. Fortunately, my training under Daisy Fickensher allowed me to keep up. The setting was rather formal, compared to our own times. In those days, students didn't come to school in jeans and T-shirts. The girls were all beautifully dressed. The boys wore suits to class, or jackets and ties. Shoes were highly polished. When we would go to rehearsals during warmer seasons of the year, we boys were allowed to remove our jackets.

Like many of my fellow students, I determined to pick the brains of all the wonderful teachers at the Peabody. There were plenty of great teachers and musicians to consult. My piano teacher and mentor Austin Conradi, for instance. Henry Cowell, the great American modernist composer and teacher, with whom I studied composition and counterpoint. Clara Asherfeld, a native of Hamburg who must have been close to 90 and who had known and played for Brahms when she was a young girl in Germany. You couldn't learn much technique from her, but she was full of information about the history of music. Her classes were always crowded and we would often provoke her into telling us stories about her youth.

There also was Nicholas Nabokov, related to the author Vladimir Nabokov. Nicholas was my history instructor. And, of course, as I've already mentioned, the great violinist Oscar Shumsky, whose television performances with Glenn Gould would later make him well known and who was one of my sister's principal teachers. But the most important instructor, and probably the greatest influence on my musical life, was still to come.

About a year after I'd started at the Peabody, I was sitting outside Conradi's studio awaiting my turn at the piano. Along came a handsome, well-dressed

Welshman. He saw me sitting there. Just sitting there. He stopped. And then he strode right up to me and said, "Who are you? Where are you from? Whom are you studying with?"

When I told him that I was studying with Austin Conradi, he said, "Good, good." But his attitude seemed to be that if anyone were sitting still, there had to be something wrong. He looked at me up and down. Then he said: "You need to be practicing! Or writing! Or going to the library! But you're just sitting there!"

I had no ready answer, of course.

He paused, then asked, "How much time do you have?"

"It's almost three o'clock," I said. "I'm not due to go in until four."

"Come with me," he replied, and he briskly walked down the hall. What could I do but follow? You do what people tell you if they're teachers or professors, and this fellow certainly was, although I still didn't know his name. I followed him down the hall and up a flight of stairs. We entered a room with 15 boys and girls in it.

"You must be a baritone," he said in a low tone of voice. "Go sit over there."

Next thing I knew, I was singing in a madrigal group composed of a handpicked assemblage of voice majors and assorted musicians. My God, we started singing in four parts and in eight parts. It was exciting as hell.

My new-found teacher was touchy. He might say, for instance, "I'm not going to watch you."

"What do you mean?" I replied. "I haven't even started singing yet."

"I can see it on your face that it won't be good," he said.

Thus did I meet my second genius and mentor, William Ifor Jones. (He always went by his second name to his friends.) Born in Merthyr Tydfil, Wales, Ifor Jones had attended the Royal Academy of Music in London. He'd studied the organ with Sir Stanley Marchant and had conducted with Sir Henry Wood, the great English conductor who had popularized classical music in England with his Promenade Concerts at Royal Albert Hall back in the 1890s. Through his efforts, Wood had vastly improved the level of English taste and competence in music.

Ifor Jones had come to the United States after working at the Royal Opera House and for the British National Opera Company. Here in America, he conducted the New Chamber Orchestra in Philadelphia and the Tudor Singers in Bethlehem, Pennsylvania. He taught at the Peabody, among other places. By 1939, he'd become the third conductor of the acclaimed Bach Choir and Festival in Bethlehem.

We Peabody students loved this man, absolutely adored him, for his brilliance and for his dedication. Of course, he treated us like crap. But what were we going to do? He called me Manos for 15 years. It took 15 more years for me to work up the nerve to address him by his first name and to say, "Ifor, how are you?" And that had been at the urging of his wife, Lillian Knowles, who had told me, "For goodness sake, call him Ifor!"

Jones was a very astute, well-mannered, sophisticated, and beautifully clothed Brit. He was like a god to us students, and drew more than a few passes from the women in our midst. Right underneath his looks and his charm lay stupendous musical talent. Even the great Sir Henry Wood had predicted that Jones and another student of Wood's, Leopold Stokowski, would become the two conductors to carry on the torch for him.

At the Peabody Conservatory, Ifor Jones gave me a new understanding of choral and orchestral music, and helped me get light years ahead with my conducting. At that time, conducting, after piano, was my second musical love.

After working on my conducting technique for a long time, I finally told Jones that I wanted to actually conduct at a real public event. He consented to let me conduct one of the performances that he'd scheduled at the Peabody, a performance of Bach cantatas. The singers were from the madrigal group he'd put me in and the players were professionals, so there were no problems. I loved it.

Although Jones could be harsh—the truth can be that way—he was also considerate of my feelings when he taught me about conducting. He wasn't like the great but temperamental Italian conductor Arturo Toscanini, who, frustrated by his lack of command of English, would call you every dirty word in Italian, French, and German that he couldn't think of in English. Jones wouldn't pull me over publicly and dress me down. He'd talk to me quietly and firmly, but privately. The most important thing he taught me about conducting is that you can't conduct everybody's mind. You have to be more general as a conductor because the music can get complicated and go in all different directions. Half the orchestra may be playing at 6:8 time while the other half might be playing 4:4 time.

"My God," I asked, after an early attempt at conducting. "How do you do this?"

"You'll have to find a common denominator and hit the downbeat," he said. "The rest will fall into place."

I struggled as a student conductor until he opened my eyes to that simple mathematical concept. That basic idea, of breaking down complicated pieces of music to their simplest elements, took the fear out of a lot of things. Beyond that, he taught me not only to have confidence in myself, but in my players. They are professionals, he said. He explained that I didn't have to give the players every single note to play as long as I gave them a clear sign of where I was in the score. Because that is basically what musicians are looking for. They're searching for that downbeat. Everything else is almost superfluous. "They play their instruments better than you do," Jones liked to remind me. Until I finally understood, conducting an orchestra had seemed incredibly difficult. By breaking conducting down into its essential components, Jones managed to make it comprehensible.

As I studied at the Peabody in Baltimore, I continued to expand my musical horizons in Washington. At the age of 17, I founded the New Washington Sinfonietta, an orchestra of 65 players with a standard repertoire. It was a way for me to grow very slowly, to try conducting on my own. It was an extracurricular pursuit encouraged by my mentor Jones.

I also joined the Washington Choral Society as a member of its big chorus of 150 singers. We'd sing things like Handel's *Messiah*. Typically, the National Symphony Orchestra accompanied us. But one day, on short notice, I learned that the orchestra would be out of town on the weekend of a performance we had coming up. I talked to the choral society's conductor, Louis Potter, and told him that my grandly named New Washington Sinfonietta practiced on Monday nights, and that we'd be happy to pinch-hit for the National Symphony Orchestra if he were amenable. (How I came up with that name I don't really know. Despite its impressive sound, sinfonietta just means small symphony. What did I know?)

Potter came over on Monday to check out our rehearsal. Apparently, we passed muster. He called me later at home and said, "You're sure you'll have time for me?" Hardly able to conceal my excitement, I replied, "Yes, of course. It's all yours."

Among friends in Washington who played the oboe, violin, cello, and other instruments, I somehow scraped together enough troops for a performance. I still have the original program. It says: "The Washington Choral Society, Louis Potter conducting the New Washington Sinfonietta; George Manos directing." That was a tad optimistic. Actually, Potter did just about everything. I sang in the chorus.

That was really our little sinfonietta's sole performance, but it was a good one, in Constitution Hall, Washington's center for major musical events. Although unseasoned, the players were young and full of energy, and gave a good account of themselves. The performance was well received.

Most of the time, we just practiced Monday nights. I'd walk in to rehearsals with a ton of music under my arm and get a chance to practice and feel what it was like to be a maestro. What did it feel like? It was exhilarating! The players got to play and practice, and they loved it. I loved it as well. The rehearsals focused my talents as a conductor and gave me confidence.

A couple of years later, in 1947, I joined the Washington Oratorio Society. I also began to expand my musical training beyond Baltimore, to Yale in New Haven and to the Juilliard School in New York. At Yale, I sat in on courses given by Paul Hindemith, the German-born composer, violinist, and conductor who had immigrated to the United States in 1940. I'd gone up to Yale for a week or so with a pianist friend of mine named Seymour Fink. We'd both studied at the Peabody under Austin Conradi, who'd remarked that if he could somehow have joined the two of us into one, he would have created one of the greatest American pianists ever.

Fink studied piano at Yale with the fine teachers there, and harpsichord with the great Wanda Landowski. When he brought me to his classes, I was amazed to be in the presence of such giants, especially the great Hindemith, whom I'd only read about in books, magazines, and newspapers, and heard on recordings. Hindemith's opera and symphony, *Mathis der Maler*, were tremendously popular.

When I got back to Baltimore, I told Ifor Jones about Hindemith. "Wouldn't it be nice," Jones said, "if we could give an all-Hindemith concert here at the Peabody. He writes beautiful songs, and we have a nice contralto here. We have the famous Fritz Kroll teaching violin with his quartet, and he can play one of the concertos."

So we invited Hindemith down to Baltimore, and he accepted. He didn't have to work hard at all, as we'd rehearsed everything. We set him up in a hotel, got all the troops together, and rehearsed one last time with Hindemith. I sang in a couple of pieces. It was exciting to be under the hand of the great man himself, who was widely considered to be one of the greatest living composers. The concert was a smashing success.

Hindemith didn't look or act the part of the maestro. He was past middle age. He was short, pudgy, and his white hair was thinning. For lunch he'd have his corned-beef sandwich and a beer. His wife was a typical German hausfrau.

But he was disgustingly brilliant. He was witty and he knew all the answers. He had an amazing mathematical and musical mind. At Yale, he taught in a studio with blackboards on all four walls. When I was there with my friend Fink, Hindemith told the class, "Today, we're going to write a three-part fugue." He called out to anyone for a note. Each of us gave one in turn. He'd either accept it or reject it. If he rejected it, he'd see very clearly that it wouldn't work long before any of us could. "Later on, this won't work," he'd say. He could see how any note might affect the end and the whole of the composition, even from the start. He was like a chess grand master thinking 50 moves ahead. Before we knew it, he'd gone around the four walls of the room and finished the fugue. We all felt very privileged to be in his class. He didn't seem to mind at all that I sat in.

While I studied at the Peabody, I also attended the Juilliard a couple of times a month. But I rarely stayed overnight when I visited New York. When I did, I'd find shelter at one of the school's residence halls. I got to know my colleagues there, and I learned a lot about the metropolis from them. It was a pleasure for me to explore the big city. To me, the Waldorf-Astoria was one of the most glamorous hotels in the world. I was amazed to find out that it cost ten dollars a night to stay there—a princely sum in those days.

I started at the Peabody Conservatory in 1944, and didn't graduate until 1952. I wanted to benefit as much as possible from the wisdom and technique of Jones, Conradi, and the other great teachers there. Gleaning as much information as possible from the experienced and the wise was something I'd learned from my paternal grandfather, for whom I was named. This grandfather had been my main mentor all through life. I used to tell him that I wanted to be just like him when I grew up—perfect.

"When you die, that's when you're perfect," he told me. "But you're going to have a hell of a time getting there."

All the teachers at the Peabody were performing music in public. Some, like Henry Cowell, were composing and publishing music also. Cowell was one of America's most distinguished composers. I studied counterpoint and composition with him. It was a one-on-one class—common at the Peabody. I'd go into Cowell's studio-office, which had two Steinways. Sometimes I'd play him my compositions, or he'd play me his. More often we'd discuss musical theory and philosophy. At the time, I was fascinated with the Greek Orthodox Church and Byzantine chants. He was interested too, because he'd done some Middle Eastern studies. We had great fun trying to analyze the Byzantine chants, but finally decided that we really couldn't. You could analyze a Gregorian chant, because by the point in history that the Gregorian chant became stabilized, it had its own rules. Not so with the Byzantine. It was not that well organized. There were no rules to follow. No counterpoint at all. The lack of rules made it interesting to treat in its own way, and I wrote a couple of liturgies that were used in some Greek churches. I gave one of the Greek tunes to Cowell to work on. At our next meeting he said he couldn't do it. We had a laugh over that.

Cowell was a quiet, self-effacing man with a professorial air. Short and balding, he walked very slowly, as if lost in deep thought. He was in late middle age when I studied with him, and was already well known for his symphonies and fuguing tunes and hymns. The main thing he taught me was to be myself. Not to try to copy anybody. To be as original as possible. He encouraged me to believe in myself.

I tried to be original. But it was awfully hard in those days, when I was young. There were strong influences in the air, like Aaron Copland and the French composer Francis Poulenc. I wrote a *Missa Brevis* that was reminiscent of Poulenc's work. I suppose it's just as hard for students today not to be influenced by greatness. And perhaps not such a bad thing, when starting out, at least.

At the Peabody, I learned counterpoint, the literature of music, the history of music, and the science of music. I had to cram a lot, because I had very little academic background in music. What really saved me were the basics that the wonderful Daisy Fickensher had taught me when I'd been her piano student in Washington. We had to take ensemble lessons at the Peabody, and I had to play piano for trios and quartets. Fickensher had already put me through that, so I was never totally lost.

It still took me about a year to catch on, however, under Conradi's watchful piano coaching. It was as if he were sitting there at his piano, watching me at mine, and waiting to see if a light bulb would come on. Every time that man would play, I'd be devastated. I'd think, my God, I'll never be able to do that!

I mentioned this to a friend at Juilliard, and asked him how to solve the problem. "Very simple," he said. "Just do it." In other words, practice a lot. My Juilliard friend gave me another useful piece of advice: "When you study, go slow so that you won't make mistakes. Go so slowly that there's some underlying tempo. If you're trying to play a piece and all you see are thousands of black notes, you're never going to do it. But if you take the tempo down to one beat every five seconds, that gives the eye time to see and the brain time to put together directions and send them to your fingertips."

And that's how I learned. So many kids today want to perform immediately. They don't want to take lessons. They want to sit down at the piano and play. You can't do it that way. You have to learn to respect the instrument and what it can do. You have to study and understand the composer who writes for that instrument. That takes time. Decades. And commitment. Those are lessons that I have never forgotten.

My teachers, though brilliant, also gave me a certain amount of independence, which was crucial to making my way in the world. In fact, they encouraged me to get out into the world, beyond the school's boundaries. One day, for instance, Jones told me, "You need to conduct something. An apprenticeship."

Any moment he's going to invite me to conduct some prestigious musical assemblage, I thought.

"Where?" I finally asked after a heavy silence.

"I don't know!" he thundered. "Go out and get one!"

It may seem harsh, but Jones's attitude forced me to learn to fend for myself in the competitive world of music. So I went out and found my own work. And that's exactly what I've been doing up to the present day. Somehow, by hook or by crook, I've always found things to do.

One job that I didn't want seemed to be looming in 1948, as tensions between the United States, the Soviet Union, the People's Republic of China, and North Korea continued to grow. Unwanted employment seemed imminent: that is, service in the U.S. Army via a draft. I love this country, which has been very good to me. But I saw myself as an artist rather than a soldier. I just wasn't cut out for military service.

My brother couldn't go into the service because he suffered from various physical ailments. But I was healthy. I had a draft card and a number. Men were already being called up from school. It seemed inevitable that I'd get called and maybe wind up dead in Korea or somewhere else.

That's when my father again fell back on his extensive connections, as he had when putting an end to the boxing matches my brother and I had staged in Greensboro. My father had a close friend named Harry Robinson who was a sergeant in the U.S. Marines. Harry was stationed in Washington, and was privy to lots of Marine scuttlebutt. One day he came to our house and told us that the Marine Corps was looking for an accompanist for its musical band and orchestra, the Marine Band. This might be my ticket into the armed forces but away from the battlefield.

The Marine Band, also known as the President's Own, had a long and distinguished history. It was created by Congress in 1798 under an act signed by President John Adams in Philadelphia, then the nation's capital. The band played its first public concert in Washington two years later, on a hill overlooking the Potomac River near where the Lincoln Memorial now stands. On March 4, 1801, the band performed for Thomas Jefferson's inaugural. It has played at every presidential inaugural since. Its most famous member may be John Philip Sousa, who was the band's leader from 1880 to 1892. In the 1940s, the Marine Band played at the White House, in public in Washington, and on tour, and it still does so. It gives more than 500 concerts a year.

My father's Marine friend, Harry, told me to call the Marine Band's office and go over for an audition, which I did. In fact, I went there the next day. I auditioned on piano for the Marine Band's director, Col. William F. Santelmann, and he approved. I became a Marine, if an unlikely one, within 24 hours. Within a few weeks, my life would undergo even more dramatic changes.

3

The President's Own

Col. William F. Santelmann, the Marine Band's 21st director, did not look particularly imposing. He was a short, middle-aged man who was losing his hair.

But he could be something of a Prussian as a commanding officer. His father, Capt. William H. Santelmann, had been a director of the Marine Band years earlier. The younger Santelmann, born in Washington, had begun studying the violin at the age of six. He'd attended the same high school in Washington as I—McKinley—although years earlier. Then he'd gone off to study at the Washington School of Music and the New England Conservatory of Music in Boston.

Santelmann joined the Marine Band in 1923 as a violinist after a second audition. His father had rejected him based upon his first audition a few months earlier. The son remained, in my opinion, a poor musician when I joined the Marine Band in the summer of 1948. He had no real knowledge of good musicianship. But he had the gift of gab, and he knew how to network. Like a lot of successful people in government and business, he knew how to endear himself to others, especially those in power who could do him some good. He worked his way up through the ranks and became director in 1940, a position that he occupied until 1955.

Santelmann could be charming when he wanted, but he could also be imperious, and the latter was his more usual mode. He was an opinionated SOB, really, and used his ego and position to bully those below him. If you questioned the reasons why or how he was doing things, he'd usually reply, "Because I say so," and leave it at that.

Unlike an orchestra, a band doesn't have stringed instruments. In those days, when I joined, the Marine Band was unique because it could perform as band or orchestra. It could make the switch because many of its members could play two instruments. Nowadays, it's different. The organization has a separate band and orchestra.

One of the first things Santelmann wanted me to do was to learn to play the harp. I protested that I had my hands quite full with the piano. He replied that he needed a harpist and that, anyway, the harp was like the piano. Well, that was just stupid. The harp is not a piano.

But one day I returned home after a rehearsal and found a Lyon & Healy harp from Chicago sitting there. On it was a note from Col. Santelmann saying, "Learn this." That was silly. It takes a professional harpist just as long to master the harp as it takes a pianist to master the piano.

The harp sat in my house for six months. I didn't even try it. I had no interest in becoming a harpist. And, anyway, I didn't want to lug the thing around.

One day at morning rehearsal at Marine Barracks at Eighth and I streets in Southeast Washington, Col. Santelmann told me that I would be playing the harp at the next orchestral concert. He planned to do the *Peer Gynt Suite* by Grieg; a harp solo begins one of the movements.

I agreed, but with no pleasure. Col. Santelmann sent a truck over to the house to bring the harp down to Marine Barracks. Just for laughs, I'd learned how to play the first two chords. Every man in the orchestra was waiting for the situation to develop at rehearsal. And it did. When Col. Santelmann raised his baton, I began playing the introduction. My fellow musicians began shuffling their feet and applauding. Then I stopped. I said, "Colonel, that's as far as I go."

He was upset, but managed to contain himself. He got the message. He put an ad in the newspaper for a harpist and found a good one.

Many of the members of the band were extremely talented musicians, although some of the older salts, who had served for 20 or 25 years or more, could be a bit gruff and left something to be desired in their musicianship. But there were two younger players, both with the last name of Berkman (although they were unrelated), who were outstanding. Roy Berkman, who was about my age, 18 or 19, had studied violin with the great violin teacher Tosha Seidel, himself a former student of the great Leopold Auer of Russia. This Berkman kid played like a house on fire. I was never so impressed with anybody.

The other Berkman, John, came down from Connecticut to audition on violin and piano. The Marine Band needed a second pianist because there was more work than I could handle on my own. John Berkman played the Brahms *Violin Concerto* at his audition, and then the Tchaikovsky *Concerto*. He did both beautifully. After knocking off the violin concertos, he sat down at the Steinway grand piano we had at Marine Barracks and played Rachmaninoff's *Third Piano Concerto*. All of these were high peaks of music. He conquered them as if he were just walking up a hill for a picnic. He knocked our socks off. And he was a nice guy too. Nearly all of us in the band became close friends.

I'd thought that music and the military were a strange combination, but the pairing worked well for me. I only earned $200 a month or so as a soldier, but I was for the most part a Marine in name only. I didn't have to go to boot camp. As a piano soloist, I didn't even have to perform at many concerts or attend many rehearsals. I was especially happy about the latter, as rehearsals took place at 9 a.m. sharp at Marine Barracks, and I have never been a morning person. My schedule was so loose, in fact, that I continued attending classes at the Peabody and the Juilliard during my four years in the Marines.

There were still some military requirements to fulfill, however. The drum major, who in dress uniform wore an impressively tall bearskin hat, took to instructing me in how to march properly. And I had to study the *Marine Corps Manual* to learn the proper procedures and protocol for moving about in the organization and presenting it to the world.

Uniforms were another requirement of service. One type—the uniform we usually wore—consisted of dress blues: a dark navy-blue jacket and navy-blue pants with white and red stripes on the sides. The jacket had gold buttons. There was also a more glamorous uniform that we put on for tonier evening performances. These were fire-engine red with high collars. I called them the Austrian court uniforms. Nobody else wore them, and nobody else wears them today.

Instead of being sent to boot camp, like the typical Marine recruit, I took a train to Philadelphia, where tailors measured and fussed over me to prepare my special uniforms. Shortly after I returned to Washington, I heard a call for me over the intercom at Marine Barracks: "Staff Sergeant Manos, report to the director's office." Another benefit of my acceptance to the band was that I had been made a staff sergeant right away, rather than having to enter the service as a lowly private via the draft.

I walked upstairs to Col. Santelmann's office, worrying about whether I would stand at attention and salute him right, and about what he had in store for me. I wondered what the hell I'd done now. This is common thinking for the military freshman.

I waited in Col. Santelmann's outer office until I was called in. My commanding officer began speaking quite casually to me as he straightened papers on his desk.

"Manos," he said, "how would you like to take a cruise?"

Col. Santelmann's proposition didn't really register. I thought jokingly to myself that the Marine Corps must really appreciate me if it was offering me a vacation cruise so soon after enlisting.

"On the yacht *U.S.S. Williamsburg*," Col. Santelmann added.

I gave him a blank, bovine stare.

"The presidential yacht, Manos!" he said, as if instructing an ignorant youth.

I smiled. I thought he was being facetious. But I soon found out otherwise. President Harry S. Truman planned to take a ten-day vacation cruise down the Potomac River and into the Delaware and Chesapeake bays beginning August 20. The president wanted to have a piano player come along to play for him and his guests. Or course, I had no choice but to obey my C.O. and, indirectly, at least, my commander in chief. Scarcely a month after joining the Marine Band, I would be escorting the president of the United States on a river and sea cruise as his personal pianist. (My actual date of enlistment had been July 22.)

In the few days that I had to prepare for the trip, I began to wonder. What type of music did the president like? I knew that he was musically knowledgeable. As a struggling student, when I'd been able to scrape up the cash to attend performances by some of the greats who played at Constitution Hall, I'd often seen Truman, as vice president and later, as president, sitting in Box 13, the presidential box. Usually he was accompanied by his wife, Bess, and his daughter, Margaret, herself an aspiring singer. Many great politicians have enjoyed music and attended concerts, of course. But the thing that impressed me about Truman was that he brought along a score to these performances. You could see him following the music on the score throughout the concert.

That really should have been no surprise. As Truman biographers and interviewers like David McCullough and Merle Miller have recorded, Truman had hopes of becoming a concert pianist when he was growing up in Missouri. (Truman joked in Miller's book *Plain Speaking* that as a boy he'd wanted to become a piano player in a whorehouse or a politician, and added, as a punch line, that there really wasn't much difference between the two.)

As a youth, Truman had often attended classical concerts in Kansas City, near his home in Independence. He'd studied piano under a teacher named Grace White, herself a former pupil of an outstanding American pianist named Fannie Bloomfield Zeisler. When the great Polish pianist and politician Ignacy Jan Paderewski stopped in Kansas City to perform during a cross-country tour, White took the young Truman backstage to meet the great man. Truman had never forgotten that experience.

Boyhood friends of the president recalled that they'd always seen a music roll under his arms in those days. Truman particularly liked Mozart, Beethoven, and Chopin. His musical education had really started with a $200 upright Kimball piano that his father, John, had bought when the boy was 11, just after the family had moved into a new house in a better neighborhood in Independence.

Although he'd given up his dream of becoming a concert pianist, Truman had continued to play as an adult, right through his political career in the U.S. Senate, to the vice presidency, and into the White House. Even as president, he'd play his Steinway in the White House. Or he might play on the campaign trail—on a piano in a hotel in Buffalo, New York, at one in the morning, for instance. Music was a source of joy and solace and relaxation for Truman, an ideal, poetic statement of "things as they ought to be and not as they are," as he'd once written of music as a youth.

It took me years to learn all this about the president's musical tastes and background, of course. But to prepare for the trip, I made as many inquiries among friends and officers about his musical preferences as I could. I got some inkling of the president's musical leanings, though nowhere near the understanding of his great love of music that I gained through the coming years of playing for him. I gathered all of my music books, from Bach to Gershwin, put them in a briefcase, and prepared to go down to the Washington Navy Yard. The *Williamsburg* was berthed at Pier One, awaiting the president and his retinue. It was just a short walk for me down the street from Marine Barracks.

There was another problem, however. My uniforms—the dress blues and the red Austrian court numbers—had not yet arrived from Philadelphia. I'd have to borrow clothes from other members of the band. Excited about the news, they already were asking me to make special requests for favors from my influential new boss, the president. I handled their supplications diplomatically, pointing out that while I appreciated the loan of their uniforms, the president doubtless had better things to do than to think about the personal problems of members of the Marine Band.

Pretty soon, I'd assembled a wardrobe that I thought could get me through the cruise, at least. I got a dress-blues uniform from a fellow band member who was close to my size. The red Austrian court get-up, also somewhat ill fitting, came from another band member. I found some summer-weight khakis that Marines sometimes wear, though these had no stripes.

When I got to the Navy Yard's main gate, a Marine guard stopped me and hollered, "You're out of proper uniform, Marine!" He didn't know about the

Marine Band, apparently, nor could he understand what I was doing in the Navy Yard, or the strange look of my not-quite-regulation uniform.

"Where do you think you're going? Where's your white belt?" he said.

When I told him that I was going to see the president, a look of grave concern crossed his face. He called the officer of the day, who eyed me with equal suspicion.

Fortunately, I'd been provided with an identification card at Marine Barracks. That, combined with a call or two to Henderson Hall, the Marine headquarters in Arlington, Virginia, and to Col. Santelmann, my commanding officer, convinced the suspicious Marines that I was at the Navy Yard on legitimate business. I never persuaded them that I was a sergeant rather than a private, however. That may be the source of the confusion in the official log of the ensuing cruise, which lists me as Private George Manos.

My troubles didn't quite end after I got through the gate. Before the big day, Col. Santelmann and his drum major had patiently coached me, obviously a landlubber and not even much of a soldier, in the correct way to board a ship. Despite the cram course in maritime protocol, I was still a bit apprehensive by the time I reached the *Williamsburg*. I loitered about next to the ship long enough to watch two or three sailors go up the gangway. They seemed to do it easily, although I couldn't hear if they'd requested formal permission to board the ship, as Col. Santelmann and the drum major had instructed me to do.

Finally, I screwed up my courage, strode up the gangway, saluted the colors, and turned to the officer of the deck to make my formal request. This old salt obviously knew a greenhorn when he saw one. "Come aboard!" he roared. Looking around, I noticed that few of the crew members evinced the snap and formality that I'd affected. In fact, some seemed to be snickering. I presented my orders to the executive officer and was assigned to quarters, where I retired immediately and somewhat sheepishly.

After I stowed my bags in the crew's quarters, I looked over the ship. The *Williamsburg* was indeed impressive, as a presidential yacht should be. She was a beauty, meticulously finished and elegantly furnished, like a real yacht. Nearly 244 feet long, with a steel hull, she had been laid down March 19, 1930, as the private yacht *Aras II* at the Bath Iron Works in Bath, Maine. The U.S. Navy had acquired her in April 1941 and converted her for naval service at the Brewer Drydock in Brooklyn, New York. Renamed the *Williamsburg*, she served during World War II as a gunboat and then as a general communications vessel.

Truman had her designated as the presidential yacht in November 1945, preferring her roomy accommodations to the smaller *Potomac*, the presidential yacht of his predecessor, President Roosevelt. Truman used the *Williamsburg* as a place to relax and also as a remote office where he could work outside the pressure and constant interruptions of Washington. Often he'd take key aides along on his cruises, which could range from short trips down the Potomac to longer excursions into the Chesapeake and Delaware bays. Sometimes the *Williamsburg* would even make runs up to New England or to Bermuda.

As a presidential yacht, the *Williamsburg* had nearly 200 crew members, including white-jacketed Filipinos who served as waiters in the president's dining room in the main saloon on the main deck. Each of the yacht's two saloons was richly paneled and furnished.

I'm sad to note that this fine ship has since wound up as a derelict. After she was decommissioned in 1953, the *Williamsburg* was transferred to the National Science Foundation, renamed the *Anton Bruun*, and used for oceanographic study until she was seriously damaged in 1968. Later renamed the *Williamsburg* again, she went through a variety of owners and was last reported to be rusting away in Rapallo, Italy. There is some glimmer of hope for her preservation, however. Lloyd's Yacht and Ship Brokers of Fort Lauderdale, Florida, had her listed for sale recently at an asking price of $12 million. It was estimated on the yacht broker's Web site announcing the *Williamsburg's* availability that restoration would cost millions more, however.

After all the crew had come aboard, President Truman arrived, accompanied by a contingent of six Secret Service men and several close aides: Admiral William Leahy, the United States' first fleet admiral and also a wise political counselor; Clark Clifford, the president's special counsel; Major Gen. Harry M. Vaughan, military aide; John R. Steelman, assistant to the president; Charles G. Ross, the president's press secretary (who had been a classmate of the president and his future wife at Independence High School); and Brigadier Gen. Wallace H. Graham, the president's physician and another old friend of Truman's.

"Five-star Leahy," as the president called him, had accompanied Truman to the Allied talks at the Potsdam Conference, and was a key military and political advisor. Vaughan, who had served with Truman's artillery unit in World War I, when Truman was an officer in the U.S. Army, was a garrulous, lighthearted man whom Truman liked to have around. Vaughan liked to laugh at himself as well as with others. The historian and Truman biographer Robert M. Ferrell has written that when something went wrong in the Truman White House, staffers would often say, "Cherchez le Vaughan." Gen. Graham was an old friend who'd grown up in Independence with Truman. Graham's father, also a physician, had been Truman's mother's doctor.

It was hot and humid on the deck of the *Williamsburg*, as it usually is in Washington in August. At one in the afternoon, we cast off from Pier One. Commander Donald J. MacDonald captained the ship as we made our way down the Potomac on the first leg of our trip, to Blakiston Island, a distance of 70 miles. The river escort vessel *Lenore*, under the command of Chief Quartermaster Frederick F. Stirewait, followed close behind.

We passed Mount Vernon, Indian Head Pier, Quantico Pier, and other easily recognizable landmarks. At about seven in the evening, with the temperature hovering around 83 degrees, we anchored in about seven fathoms of water a mile off Blakiston Island.

A whaleboat and lifeboat were lowered, along with the port gangway. Soon many of the crew, dressed in bathing suits, were diving into the water and splashing and frolicking. There was no air conditioning on board, and the cool, clear water off the island was a welcome relief. A little while later the *Williamsburg's* executive officer, Commander Jesse B. Bay, joined his men in the water. President Truman, clad in his bathing trunks, soon appeared on deck with Commander MacDonald and a couple of other officers. Each dove off the port gangway and swam for ten minutes or so. While swimming, Truman kept his wire-rimmed glasses on all the time. He'd had terrible eyesight since he was a boy, and he needed his glasses to find his way back to the ship, no doubt.

I was standing at the rail, enjoying the antics of the crew splashing about in the water and diving off the monkey ropes, when I was greeted by a friendly voice with a Missouri drawl that said, "You must be the piano player." It was the president. He'd changed back into his civilian clothes—for the purposes of this trip, loose-fitting slacks, a Hawaiian shirt, and a Panama hat.

I introduced myself and told the president that I was honored to be on board, and that I hoped I'd live up to his expectations as a pianist. We chatted on deck as we watched the crew swim. Mostly we talked about music, and his likes and dislikes.

Chopin was among his favorite composers, he told me. Although the lyrical Polish musician was not at the top of my list, I was impressed with the president's broad discussion of music during our chat. Even during an informal conversation, it was easy to see that he knew a lot about music. In fact, he seemed to know a lot about everything. He wasn't bragging or showing off, either. He'd just been an avid reader since he was a kid, and he'd absorbed a tremendous amount of knowledge. When he was a boy, his poor eyesight had kept him out of sports, making him something of a sissy in the eyes of some of his childhood friends. But he'd put that time to good use. He'd read through encyclopedias, histories, and biographies. Indeed, he'd ploughed through most of the contents of the Independence Library. And, of course, he'd studied piano intensely when he wasn't reading.

I was impressed by Truman's scholarship. But I'll never forget one part of our first discussion.

"You know," he said, "you don't have to like me. You don't have to vote for me. But always remember to have respect for the office of the president, no matter who's in it."

That advice, given by a man who himself was unceasingly courteous to all around him (though an aggressive fighter if he or his family were attacked), has stayed with me over the years. I'm no fan of Richard Nixon. But Truman's words came to me years later when I watched President Nixon hold a televised press conference with a group of antagonistic reporters.

President Nixon and Dan Rather had disagreed about some issue, and the two men had become testier as they sparred verbally. President Nixon finally had looked at the television newsman and said, "Mr. Rather, are you running for president?" And Rather had replied, "No, are you?" It was not the proper retort to make to a president. It made both men look small; but especially Rather.

A similar incident occurred when Eartha Kitt raised an angry complaint about insufficient efforts to help black Americans during the Johnson Administration. This was a perfectly acceptable position to hold. The only problem was that Kitt brought it up during a big lunch that Lady Bird Johnson was giving in the White House East Room for a variety of professionals. There are better places and ways to raise such issues, rather than to embarrass someone in their own home—especially so temporary though important a home as the White House.

Talking to President Truman—the Boss, as his staff called him, though never to his face—was like talking to my father. He wasn't officious or uppity in any way. But he was supremely self-confident. He was the president, and he knew it. Meeting him for the first time, I hadn't known what to expect. I'd thought that such an important, busy man might be very uptight and hurried. But he was very relaxed. He spoke quietly and normally, as any nice gentleman would do. He could have been a college professor, given his gentle demeanor and his broad knowledge of music, the arts, and history.

We were both pianists, so we compared notes. We liked the same composers, it turned out: the three Bs—Brahms, Beethoven, and Bach—plus Mozart and Chopin. The president was much more devoted to Chopin than I, of course. But he seemed to relax particularly well when he listened to Chopin's dreamy, glissando music.

As far as I know, I was the only solo piano player ever retained by a president of the United States to regularly play for him. Many presidents, of course, have entertained guests at receptions with trios and quartets and chamber music, or feted visitors or marked important occasions with performances by bands and orchestras. But I was the only solo pianist to perform exclusively and regularly for the president and his circle.

I think that President Truman really wanted to make use of my talents to relax, rather than entertain. My playing was a bit of an escape for him, just as some people go about their work with a radio softly playing in the background. He had a lot on his mind, after all. And he had come to the presidency by a circuitous route: a surprise addition to the Democratic ticket as Roosevelt's running mate in 1944, and then sudden ascendancy to the presidency after Roosevelt's death the next year.

After his swim and our chat, the president had dinner with his entourage in the main dining room while I softly played Chopin and other classical pieces on the little Steinway upright there. It was one of two such pianos on board, and was chosen because it took up little space. After dinner, the movie *Life with Father*, starring Irene Dunne and William Powell, was shown for the presidential party. But Truman skipped the movie and turned in early, at 9:30.

I went to bed early too, exhausted from a long day in a new environment and after my premier performance before the president. While we slept, the escort ship *Lenore* radioed the *Williamsburg* at about one in the morning that William W. Janssen, engineer third class, had complained of a severe stomach ache. After a brief radio consultation, Janssen was transferred to the *Williamsburg*, where the ship's physician (and a member of the White House staff), Commander Ashton Emerson, diagnosed acute appendicitis. The president's doctor, Gen. Graham, concurred in the diagnosis, and the medical staff performed an emergency appendectomy at 5:30 in the morning. The operation was successful, and Janssen was transferred later in the day to the Naval Hospital at the Naval Air Test Center at the *Williamsburg's* next stop, Patuxent, Maryland.

The president arose about an hour after the operation, when swimming call again was sounded for the crew. He went for another dip that morning, this time accompanied by Gen. Graham. During the 50-mile trip downriver to Patuxent later that day, we passed the yacht *Potomac*, which flew the state of Maryland's flag. The state's governor, Preston Lane, was on board the 165-foot *Potomac*, FDR's former presidential yacht, to greet us.

FDR had used the yacht so much during Washington's sultry summers that it came to be known as the Floating White House. The *Potomac* has met a happier fate than the *Williamsburg*. Though she sailed through some rough years after the state of Maryland disposed of her, and was confiscated by the federal Drug Enforcement Agency in California during a narcotics operation in 1980, she has since been purchased by a nonprofit group and set up as a floating museum at Jack London Square in Oakland, California.

President Truman and Governor Lane exchanged greetings by radio-telephone as we passed:

"The governor of Maryland welcomes the president of the United States to Maryland waters and the greatest natural harbor in the world."

"The president appreciates most highly the welcome of the governor of Maryland to his great harbor. He hopes that at some future date the governor may take a cruise with the president."

After docking at Patuxent, we discharged our recovering patient, engineer third-class Janssen, and received mail flown out to Patuxent from the White House. Liberty call sounded at 2:15 in the afternoon for the crew. Some idea of the informality of these cruises may be gained from the fact that several members of the Secret Service went ashore for a game of golf, as did some of the president's inner circle.

That evening, around seven, we stood out into Chesapeake Bay. Our next stop was to be Annapolis, about 50 miles away. I played piano again for the president and his entourage during dinner, as I would continue to do through the trip. I'd also play occasionally at lunch, when the heat wasn't too oppressive. But cool, foggy mornings often were followed by days that got hotter as the trip continued.

Sunday morning, we anchored just off the United States Naval Academy at Annapolis. The *Lenore* dropped anchor nearby, and a Navy crash boat (typically used to rescue downed fliers) patrolled the waters around us as a security measure. The president, accompanied by Gen. Graham, Admiral Leahy, and other members of his party, used a barge supplied by Rear Admiral James L. Holloway Jr., superintendent of the academy, to go ashore.

Admiral Holloway greeted the presidential party at the landing, then walked with them a quarter-mile to the academy's chapel. After stopping on the chapel's steps to watch the brigade of midshipmen march into the building, the president and his party followed to attend services conducted by Commander E.P. Buebens, the academy's chaplain. Afterward, the president shook hands with the chaplain and complimented him on the service. Then Admiral Holloway introduced the president to Midshipman John Paul Jones. The president told Jones that he hoped he'd live up to his illustrious namesake, the American Revolutionary War naval hero, and that he was sure he would.

Newspaper reporters and photographers recorded the president's visit onshore. Later, Ernest V. Vaccaro, whom everyone called Tony, radio-telephoned the president's press secretary. Vaccaro, a reporter with the Associated Press, told Ross that some White House correspondents had chartered a cabin cruiser, the *Wanderer*, at Solomon's Island, Maryland, and would follow the *Williamsburg* on the next leg of the trip. Ten reporters, including representatives of the *New York Times*, *New York News*, *Washington Evening Star*, *Baltimore Sun*, CBS, NBC, and Fox Movietone News, would be aboard the *Wanderer*. Ross arranged for twice-daily press briefings from his office. The president often would chat informally with the reporters on the *Williamsburg's* fantail or ashore during stops.

That night, at dinner, I was summoned again to play for the president and his party. The president arrived last, and sat nearest me and the piano. When the signal was given to me, I played softly, for about an hour, until the president and his colleagues adjourned to watch the movie *Key Largo*. The choice seemed appropriate, given the nautical setting and the president's love of the Florida Keys. During his administration, Truman often spent time in Key West at what came to be called the Little White House at the naval base there.

When I played during these meals, I of course overheard the conversation of Truman and his guests. Much of it was over my head as a still very young man, although I do recall a certain amount of good-natured cussing and also some unflattering declamations on various of Washington's political personalities. But I decided that such conversations were strictly confidential, and never related them to anyone. Nor will I here. For Truman, this trip was as much about business as about pleasure. He was conferring with some of his smartest men, like Clifford and Leahy, and with his press and political experts, like Leahy and Ross, about the Whistle-Stop Strategy he would soon undertake when the 1948 presidential election shifted into high gear.

Truman was considered the absolute underdog that year. Much of the press seemed to have reached the conclusion that his modesty signified a lack of resolve and leadership. They completely underestimated him. He was not only a firm and decisive leader. He also was an extremely intelligent and well-read man, with a quick and incisive mind. Although many people doubted he could win the election, he seemed to be supremely confident that he would.

Years later, after Truman's death, many of his friends and also the reporters who covered him convened at the National Press Club to officially dedicate the bar there as the Truman Lounge in his memory. It was the place where Truman had the famous picture taken of him sitting at the piano and grinning while Lauren Bacall sat above him and dangled her legs over the side of the piano. A smart public-relations man had seen Truman sitting at the piano and had quickly plopped Bacall there for a photograph, much to the pleasure of everybody, with the exception of Truman's wife.

Old friends and acquaintances, along with many reporters and editors who knew Truman, reminisced about the Boss at the dedication. I gave a short talk about my musical days with Truman, and later I played piano in the lounge. Clark Clifford told a memorable story that evening illustrating Truman's keen powers of observation. Clifford had debarked from Truman's train during the Whistle-Stop Tour at a small town in Iowa to pick up the latest issue of *Time* magazine. When Clifford looked at the magazine's cover, he was horrified to see that *Time* was touting a story in which 100 so-called political experts had agreed unanimously that the Republican candidate, Thomas E. Dewey, would handily defeat Truman in November. Clifford bought the magazine anyway, and hid it under his coat so the Boss wouldn't see it. He tried to keep it hidden from Truman as he got back in the car with him. But he couldn't deceive the president, who asked to look at it.

After skimming the story, the president told Clifford not to worry.

"I know every one of those men," Truman assured his aide. "Not one of them has sense enough to pound sand down a rat hole."

Clifford's story, which perfectly captured Truman's common sense, confidence, and mental sharpness, drew howls of approval and laughter that evening at the National Press Club.

The details of the Whistle-Stop Tour strategy that these men worked out during the *Williamsburg* trip proved to be amazingly effective. In a way, it was classic Truman style. His campaign strategy counted on personal human contact rather than money to get his populist points across. On his train trip across the country, Truman would stop and deliver from the back of his train a seemingly impromptu speech, followed by applause and cries of "Give 'em hell, Harry!" from the big crowds that gathered. I'm sure that the meat of these speeches was cooked up on board the *Williamsburg*.

Today, in our media-soaked world, such a strategy wouldn't pay off. But in Truman's time, it worked perfectly, as shown by another famous photograph: the one of him holding a copy of the *Chicago Daily Tribune* announcing "Dewey Defeats Truman" on the day that Truman learned he'd actually won his next four years in office.

The weather continued hot for the rest of our cruise, except for the occasional foggy morning. Sometimes it became so difficult to see that we had to drop anchor and wait for the fog to lift. Those were the days before electronic navigation, after all. Once a pilot came aboard the *Williamsburg* and helped us find our way through the Chesapeake.

When we entered the Chesapeake and Delaware Canal, throngs of people lined the shore, piers, and bridges, and shouted greetings at us. Small boats followed in our wake, their occupants waving. The sun had come out again, and the president and his entourage lounged on the sun deck in their bathing suits. Truman cheerfully returned the salutations he got from shore.

We passed through the Delaware Bay, around Cape Henlopen, and out into the open Atlantic. The *Wanderer* elected not to follow us out to sea, although William Booth, a reporter for *Time*, did hitch a ride with the *U.S.S. Joseph P. Kennedy Jr.*, a destroyer that accompanied us in open water.

The trip continued in the same relaxed fashion, with nightly piano playing at dinner for the president and his aides, followed by popular movies, until we reached the Naval Mine Depot on the James River in Virginia.

Truman was a great walker. Years earlier, his physician, Gen. Graham, had instructed him to take a brisk walk for a couple of miles every day before breakfast. This Truman did faithfully, whether on land or at sea. The heat was no problem because, ever the Missouri farmer, he arose every day at about 5:30 a.m. On board the *Williamsburg*, he'd stride around the ship in the mornings at the good doctor's recommended pace of 120 steps per minute.

Occasionally Truman would take such walks on shore when we called at different ports. One such outing came at the mine depot, where he gave the Secret Service a bit of a scare. I was standing on deck taking in the view when I heard the words "United States ... United States" come over the intercom. I asked an officer nearby what that meant. He told me that it was code, and meant that the president was unescorted and could be in danger. He pointed to shore. There was Truman, walking stick in hand, taking a brisk and jaunty walk. He was alone. Several Secret Service men rushed down to accompany him. Truman continued to walk along, in his country-gentleman strut, as if nothing were amiss.

At Yorktown, where the *Williamsburg* docked at Pier Two, the press boat *Wanderer* had caught up with us by sailing south via the inner passage. Later that day, ten reporters came aboard the *Williamsburg* and squatted on the fantail, where Truman held an impromptu press conference.

The president was a very down-to-earth Democrat, and spoke easily with the press in his Missouri twang. He had the gift of gab, and he loved to talk with reporters. It was a way for him not only to get his views across, but to get an idea of what the populace was thinking. Truman often complained in letters to friends about press coverage. But mainly he aimed his complaints at the wealthy press lords who owned the newspapers that attacked him—men like William Randolph Hearst, Roy Howard, and Henry Luce. These press barons merely were pushing the right-wing agenda that benefited them and their wealthy friends, he said. He took a much friendlier tone with the working press, although that didn't prevent him from lashing out in response to critical stories.

At Yorktown, we were nearly a week into the cruise, and I was running out of musical material for my performances. Every night, and sometimes during lunch, I'd don my dress blues and play for the president and his entourage. But I didn't know everything at the age of 20. (Now, 60 years later, I still don't.)

I said exactly that to Truman after he'd requested a piece by Chopin that I didn't know: "Mr. President, I don't know everything." How could I? Chopin's repertoire alone includes thousands of compositions.

Truman nodded understandingly. He gave me a five-dollar bill and told me to ride with his driver in the presidential limousine into town to buy some more of Chopin's music. "Greatest music ever written," he said as I headed out to find some more of the composer's oeuvre.

I walked down the gangway. At the bottom, a very glamorous-looking black automobile awaited me.

"Where are we near that I could find some music by Chopin to buy?" I asked the driver.

After studying me for a moment with a quizzical look, the driver said, "Portsmouth."

I peered through the window as we whizzed along the roads of coastal Virginia hoping that we'd pass a music store. Finally we did. I told the driver to stop. I went in and found a book of Chopin's music, which I bought immediately. Then we sped back to the *Williamsburg*.

I didn't know a lot of the music in that book. It's lucky that I was a good sight reader. Playing unfamiliar music for the president and his friends scared the hell out of me, but I made it through. At the end of the trip, Truman inscribed the book to me with his thanks for my playing during the cruise, and gave it to me. Recently I donated the book to the Truman Library.

Beginning with this trip, my Chopin repertoire increased dramatically. I played Chopin nocturnes, polonaises, sonatas—you name it. In fact, I was playing his *B-flat Minor Sonata* one evening on the *Williamsburg* for the president and his friends when Gen. Vaughan interrupted my performance rather grumpily, unusual for so cheerful a fellow.

"What are you playing that music for?" he demanded as he banged his hand on the table. "It's too sad!"

He was referring to the piece's famous Funeral March movement, which with its melancholy tum-tum-tee-tum-tum-tee-tum-tee-tum-tee-tum rhythm had by then become a cliché on movie soundtracks. He ordered me to stop. I said, "Well, general, I agree with you, but that's what the president wants to hear."

Truman broke in then and took the chill out of the saloon with a nice little story. He leaned over toward me from his chair at the dinner table and said, "No, that's the slow movement. It's called the Funeral March because that's its character."

He told me to play the opening movement. I banged out a few bars in the opening's agitated style.

"That's someone thinking of committing a murder," Truman said. Then he ordered me to play the beginning of the second movement, a scherzo.

"That sounds pretty rough," he said. "That's the act of violence."

"Now start the Funeral March," he said, and I did.

"That's the funeral after the attack," Truman said. "Start the last movement."

That scared the hell out of me, because it's the most difficult part of the entire composition. I got through only a few bars when Truman cut me off.

"You hear that?" he said. "That's the wind running through the tombstones."

It was a fascinating story, which I've never heard before and have never heard since. Where Truman got it, or if he devised it in his own mind, I do not know. The story calmed Gen. Vaughan, at least, and amused the rest of our party, and the dinner continued with pleasant talk and my soft piano playing, followed by cigars, drinks, and the nightly movie.

The trip continued as before, with occasional press conferences and plenty of sun bathing, swims, and working sessions for Truman and his men. The weather only got hotter as we approached Washington. The temperature reached 97 degrees on Saturday, August 28. On such steamy afternoons, the president would usually retreat to his stateroom for a nap.

Truman seemed to be in good spirits during the entire voyage. By the end, he looked fit, tanned, and well rested, even though he and his men had laid the difficult groundwork for his election campaign. A seaplane came every day to deliver and take away White House mail. Aides came and went at every port we visited.

After a return visit to Blakiston Island on Saturday for a swim, we turned around on the Potomac and headed back toward the Naval Base in Washington on Sunday. The banks of the river were lined with Sunday picnickers. The president went up on the flying bridge for an hour or so to enjoy the sun and the views. Passing Mount Vernon again, we paid the traditional honors to George Washington: The crew stood at quarters, the ship's bell tolled, and the colors were lowered to half mast while taps was played.

At four o'clock, we arrived back at Pier One, where we were met by more reporters and photographers, military aides, and relatives of some of the men on board. The president stopped on his way down the gangway to pose for photographs and to chat with reporters. Then he and his aides sped off in waiting automobiles back to the White House.

There were, of course, more cruises to come during Truman's next four years in office. I accompanied him on several. But the first one is the trip that I remember best. Mostly, it is the president who stays in my mind, and his kindness, intelligence, honesty, and strength of character. I remember him at least as much for what he was not. He was unpretentious, unhurried, and unshakable. He was a man who knew who he was; he was secure in his own skin. He never changed during the four years that I played for him.

For me, the trip was also a small historic landmark. Although various ensembles have entertained presidents aboard their yachts in the past, I was the first solo pianist to accompany a president for an entire cruise.

4

White House Pianist

Back on land, I returned to the family home—now in Bethesda, Maryland—continued my studies, and remained on call with the Marine Band. As I said, I was really a Marine in name only. I rehearsed and played only when Col. Santelmann needed a piano soloist for a performance. Otherwise, I was free to continue my studies at the Peabody Conservatory.

Besides performing occasionally with the Marine Band, I also became the announcer for many of its radio performances—a position that led me to join the National Press Club in Washington. I also traveled with the Marine Band when required. Some performances would take me only a short drive away, such as those at the Marine base in Quantico, Virginia. At other times, we'd make extended tours, for ten days or so. We got around on these trips via trains with individual sleeping compartments, much like that other band in the movie *Some Like It Hot*. I wish I had a nickel for every time I played Gershwin's "Rhapsody in Blue" during those tours.

We'd stay at hotels in the towns and cities where we played. For the younger ones among us, there was something of a playful, fraternity-house atmosphere in the band. The older salts, those who had put their 20 or 25 years into the band as a career, and who were looking forward to retirement, usually brought along a bottle or two on the trips to help pass the time. They had to have their swigs. In general, we carried on like a bunch of idiots. But we were very young, most of us.

In Washington, we played at two places on a regular basis: in the Marine Barracks itself, in the John Philip Sousa Memorial Auditorium, where there was a band shell; and in the Department of Commerce's auditorium. A lot of government buildings in Washington have auditoriums, and Commerce had a very fine one. We played there many times.

Of course, there's one other notable engagement that the Marine Band had in 1949: playing at Truman's inauguration following his surprising election victory.

It appeared to surprise everyone but Truman, at least, who'd predicted all along that he'd beat Dewey.

At less formal events where we played, I sometimes enjoyed experimenting and having a bit of fun. In high school, I'd been notorious for improvising. The kids and even many of the teachers seemed to like that when I played: What would crazy Manos come up with today?

Musical improvisation hardly began with me, of course. Great composers like Beethoven, Mozart, and Haydn had all written cadenzas as variations on themes within their works. Some of the more creative pianists throughout history used to improvise, though that's become uncommon today. But I fell prey to the habit as a youth. It was a way of thumbing my nose, though in a polite way, at the school administration.

I carried this love of improvisation on to the Marine Corps. Sometimes, if an audience liked a performance, they'd demand an encore. I might play a piece by Chopin or Bach, or a smaller bagatelle by Beethoven. Sometimes, just for the hell of it, I'd start improvising on a prelude and fugue based on the tunes of the Sousa marches. The other players in the band caught on and had a big laugh over what I was doing, because Col. Santelmann usually had no idea.

"That's fascinating," he'd say afterward. "Who wrote that?"

"Oh, you dumb ass," I'd think to myself. I did a lot of nonsense like that when I wasn't playing for Truman or during more important occasions.

As soon as he won the November election, Truman decided to have the White House gutted. The beautiful old building suffered from what the real-estate agents today like to call deferred maintenance. As an aspiring singer, Truman's daughter, Margaret, had a piano in a sitting room across the hall from her father's study in the White House. One day one of the legs of the big Steinway grand crashed through the old floor. That's when Truman decided that it was time for some badly needed renovations at the White House.

He hired Edward F. Nield to make the plans and oversee the work. Nield had designed a beautiful courthouse in Shreveport, Louisiana. Truman had seen it when he drove around the country looking for design inspirations while he was presiding judge in Kansas City, where he'd wanted to build a new courthouse. He'd asked Nield to construct a building in Kansas City similar to the one he'd created in Louisiana, and Nield had built a beauty.

To renovate the White House, Nield practically had to tear the old building apart. The interior was stripped to the walls. If you went inside, you could look up and see the sky. While the extensive renovation on the White House was taking place, Truman lived and worked in the Blair-Lee House, across Pennsylvania Avenue from the White House and just across from Lafayette Square.

The Blair-Lee House had started as two Federal-style houses built in the 19th century. Francis Preston Blair, editor of the *Washington Globe* and a member of President Andrew Jackson's Kitchen Cabinet, had built the Blair House in 1824. The historian George Bancroft is among the eminences who have stayed there. Next door, the Lee House, a handsome, red-brick building, had been built in 1856. It was the home of Rear Admiral Samuel Phillips Lee and his wife, Elizabeth Blair Lee. It had been given to the couple by Elizabeth's father, Francis Preston Blair. Lee was a member of the famous old American family that originated in Virginia, but during the Civil War he commanded the North Atlantic Blockading Squadron for the Union. Indeed, next door, in the Blair House, President Lincoln had asked but failed to convince Gen. Robert E. Lee to command the Union forces shortly after the outbreak of the Civil War.

Samuel and Elizabeth's son, Blair Lee, grew up to serve as a U.S. senator representing Maryland. He was the first U.S. senator elected by direct vote; previously, they'd been picked by state legislatures.

In 1943, President Roosevelt joined the houses together and made them a single guest house for visitors to the White House who needed overnight lodgings. Even though I was designated as the White House pianist, I never played in the White House during my four years with Truman because he worked and lived in the Blair-Lee House for almost the whole time.

Usually, I'd get a call, either from Col. Santelmann, Marine Headquarters in Arlington, or one of Truman's men, such as his aide David Stowe, a neighbor of mine in Bethesda. Someone would call and say, "The Boss is expecting you at Blair House today. Can you come down?" It was a very relaxed situation. I'd hop in a cab and ride down to Blair House.

My first time there was shortly after the president had moved in. It was in the morning, as my solo performances for the president almost always were, between 10 a.m. and noon. I had to show my Marine Band I.D. at Blair House's little guard house out front on the sidewalk. Then I was motioned to walk down a ramp to the servants' entrance downstairs. There I met a man named Howell G. Crim, who was the president's chief usher and who had a little office off the vestibule. Everything was very crowded. He was a pleasant middle-aged man who got to the point right away. He led me upstairs to the president.

My first impression of Blair House's interior: underwhelming. "How small!" I thought. Because I'd taken tours of the White House and had marveled at its enormous dining room, gorgeous ballrooms, and priceless antiques. The main salon of the Blair House was no bigger than my living room, which is in an average-sized house in Florida.

Crim showed me a Steinway upright in the corner and left me alone in the salon. I sat down at the piano and began playing. I could see the president from the corner of my eye. He was in an adjoining office, writing and sometimes talking on the telephone. Occasionally, visitors would be led in to talk to him in person. I didn't address him—he was the president, after all, and a very busy man. As on the *Williamsburg*, I played nothing too rambunctious. No Berlioz *Symphonie Fantastique*, for example. I stuck to Truman's favorites: Beethoven, Brahms, Mozart, and Chopin. I knew about his love for Chopin's moody numbers from our cruise together. Years later, in 1962, Truman affirmed his feelings about Chopin during an interview with the television journalist David Susskind. Truman told Susskind that Chopin's *A-flat Opus 42 Waltz* was his favorite piece of music; and "The Missouri Waltz" his least favorite, although it was played in his honor all the time.

I stuck to pieces that weren't too demonstrative. Chopin waltzes and mazurkas, rather than polonaises, for instance. I tried to play things that would be soothing but not distracting to the busy president. Then again, I wasn't playing on a concert grand, which could have raised the roof.

I ran through a chunk of my repertoire for an hour or so during my first appearance at the Blair-Lee House. Truman didn't acknowledge me directly—he seemed too busy—but occasionally I'd catch him looking my way, or looking up toward the ceiling and thinking, as if he were trying to identify a particular tune, or getting lost in the music. He certainly cared about the music. Among the Truman archives is one of his crowded appointment books, which chronicled his seemingly endless series of 15-minute visits with guests, including a slot so that Truman could talk with leaders of the military bands about the type of music he wanted them to play.

When it was time for me to go, a tall, imposing black man named Alonzo Fields came and motioned me to stop. Fields, who had wanted to become a singer as a youth, had ended up working on the White House staff, and had become head butler. He was sort of an African-American Jeeves: a highly intelligent, resourceful man who could fix any problem with the utmost delicacy and diplomacy. After he retired from service, he wrote a book about his experiences called *My Twenty-One Years in the White House*. In it he noted that Truman was the only president who ever took a personal interest in him and his family, and in the lives of the other servants at the White House.

I continued to play for Truman once or twice a week. It was relaxing for him—a spiritual, mental escape from the intense pressures of his job. We'd entered the atomic age, after all, and the president of the United States had become the most powerful man in the world, with its fate in his hands.

Sometimes when I'd play, with the piano pushed right up next to the president's open office door, I'd see him look up from his desk as if he were wondering what I was playing. Other times he'd walk out and ask me, then chat about the composer and the piece a bit, and return to his desk. He was always direct and to the point, and never wasted time. He couldn't afford to, in his position. But he'd grown up that way as a hard-working farmer.

At other times he'd come out and sit beside me on the piano bench and watch what I was doing. Often one of Chopin's mazurkas or minuets would trigger his interest.

Once he came out and sat down next to me and reminisced about his meeting with the great Paderewski in Kansas City when he was a boy. When his piano teacher had taken young Truman backstage to meet the great pianist and statesman after the performance, Paderewski had taught the boy how to play a turn in his famous *Minuet*. (A turn, or mordant, is a musical embellishment, dating from Baroque times, in which the pianist flits up and down from a central note. It's marked on scores by a sort of S lying on its side.)

Truman asked me if I could play the turn, and I did.

"Good," he said with a laugh. "That makes three of us."

How was Truman as a piano player? Fair. He was certainly better than another recent piano-playing president, Richard Nixon, who had the temerity to sit at a concert grand on television and attempt to play. Truman played like a man who had studied piano. He wasn't as advanced, perhaps, as we all would have liked him to have been. But he was serious about the piano and about music because he loved music.

When Truman played alongside me, he'd ask me to take over when the playing got difficult. In Paderewski's *Minuet,* for instance, he requested that I play the rest of the piece when he reached the middle section, which gets a little boisterous. Truman didn't have the octave work in his hands. After he'd got as far as he could get with Paderewski's *Minuet* or Mozart's *A-major Sonata*, he'd jump up, smile, and say, "That's all!" Then I'd finish what he'd started.

Occasionally, I'd see Mrs. Truman moving about the house. She was the woman whom Truman referred to as "the Boss." Since Truman himself was referred to by his staff as the Boss, I guess that Mrs. Truman was the Boss of Bosses. Anyway, she made no secret of the fact that she was unhappy in Washington. She'd never wanted to leave their hometown of Independence. The couple had known each other since the age of six, when they'd attended elementary school together, the future Mrs. Truman occasionally tapping her husband-to-be on the head with a pencil. He was an easy target because he sat at the desk in front of her. She was never very social and didn't get involved in Washington society or politics like some other presidents' wives.

In that way, she was completely the opposite of her predecessor, Eleanor Roosevelt. I met Mrs. Roosevelt a couple of times—once before my connection with Truman, and once in the Blair House.

During and after World War II, my sister Bes and I had toured local hospitals like Walter Reed. We'd go from ward to ward playing music for wounded servicemen. Bes played her violin, and I had a little piano on wheels that could be moved around. Occasionally my mother and my sister Helen would come along. The soldiers particularly liked having my mother there because she had a very motherly look and attitude. She'd bring a cart of candy with her, and she and Helen would hand out these treats to the patients.

It was a particularly sad sight when we went to wards where there were nothing but paraplegics. My mother and Helen would feed the kids who didn't have hands. It was heartbreaking. This program was set up by Mrs. Roosevelt, who occasionally came along.

There was no publicity, no hoopla, no hype.

The second time I met Mrs. Roosevelt, I was playing at a lunchtime reception at Blair House. A big crowd, including Mrs. Roosevelt, had squeezed into Blair House's limited space to see the president. As I was playing, one of Truman's aides came over and nudged me.

"Watch this," he said, shooting his gaze over to the living room's fireplace. There was Mrs. Roosevelt rearranging all the objects of art and knick-knacks on the mantel. I guess she wanted to get them back in the exact order they'd been in when she was in the White House.

As in everything else, President Truman was very businesslike and efficient even at these social affairs, though kindly and warm. He kept his social engagements as short and direct as his other business. I'd occasionally play in a Marine Band trio or quartet when he had cocktail parties for visiting dignitaries in the evening. Often I was accompanied by our talented violinist Roy Berkman. Guests were wise not to arrive hungry or thirsty. These events typically would start promptly at five and end promptly at six. The president would receive and greet guests in his friendly way, but once he left to attend to other business, everyone else was expected to leave.

Truman's businesslike approach extended even to royalty. Royal personages seemed to leave him completely unfazed, unlike many other Americans, then and now. When Princess Elizabeth of England and her new husband, Prince Philip, arrived in Washington for a visit—sort of a way of thanking the United States for saving their country during World War II, I think—Truman treated her like a nice visiting young lady rather than like a future queen of England. I remember him sitting down on a settee and saying, "Come over here, young lady, and sit next to me." He talked with her as he might chat with his own daughter, Margaret. Elizabeth and Philip were a good-looking young couple, and Truman treated them as such. I didn't play anything special that evening for Elizabeth and Philip. I just kept to my policy of avoiding the bombastic.

Other visiting dignitaries for whom I performed included India's Prime Minister Jawaharial Nehru, who stayed at the Blair House in 1951. He was displeased with the United States because we'd backed an arbitration plan for Kashmir, over which India and Pakistan were having a dispute. Nehru didn't openly voice his displeasure with Truman, within my earshot, at least. They seemed to chat amiably in Truman's little office. Only once did I get a sign of his temper. I heard a commotion upstairs, Nehru's voice rising, and his underlings scurrying about. "Where's my box? Where's my box?" Nehru kept demanding.

Just then the major-domo Fields glided in. What a gentleman and a gentle person! And Fields was a man who always kept his eyes and ears open. Soon he had found the missing item—a beautiful mahogany box containing the prime minister's toiletries—and had returned it to Nehru's staff. After that, Nehru became his pleasant self again: a dark-complected man with wavy gray hair who wore a cream-colored Nehru jacket and jodhpurs. He always smiled at me and the rest of Truman's staff. Of course, we smiled ourselves after we realized that the emergency of the missing box just involved a few misplaced toiletries.

It was on a quieter day, Nov. 1, 1950, that two Puerto Rican nationalists attempted to assassinate the president. I'd often worried about Truman's temporary lodgings at Blair House. His office window overlooked Pennsylvania Avenue, and anyone could have come along and taken a pot shot at him.

Truman seemed completely unafraid, however. Followed by just a small contingent of Secret Service men, he'd often walk across the street to conduct business in the West Wing or the East Wing of the White House. He'd also strut down the street sometimes to mail his own letters, which he always pasted with his own stamps, even though he could have mailed them for free. I'd occasionally accompany him on these expeditions. He'd tip his hat and greet anyone on the street who recognized him.

Gunshots don't sound the way they're portrayed in the movies. When the Puerto Rican nationalists Griselio Torresola and Oscar Collazo attacked the guards outside Blair House, we heard muffled pops outside. The attackers killed one guard, Leslie Coffelt, and wounded two others before they were subdued. During the exchange of gunfire, the guards killed Torresola and wounded Collazo.

I was playing piano when it happened. After the muffled pops, I heard someone shout, "Hit the deck! Hit the deck!" We all got down on the floor. Secret Service men rushed in and guided the president and the First Lady into an inner part of the building, away from the windows. After the excitement died down, Truman walked out and went about his business as if nothing had happened. He was, as always, completely unflappable. In fact, a little while later he was driven off to Arlington in the presidential limousine to give a speech. He had a few more Secret Service men escorting him than usual, though.

In his letters and diary, Truman later made it clear that he felt especially bad about Coffelt giving up his life to protect him. He had a plaque erected in memory of the policeman on the iron fence in front of the Blair House. It's still there today.

Collazo later was tried, convicted of Coffelt's murder, among other things, and sentenced to death. Before he left office, Truman commuted the sentence to life in prison. Decades later, President Jimmy Carter pardoned Collazo. Truman was a crazy target for the two would-be assassins to pick. He'd always been on the side of the underdog, and had supported Puerto Ricans' right to choose the political future of their island.

After the assassination attempt, life went on much as before, for Truman, at least, though he was guarded by a much heavier contingent of Secret Service men. In his diary, he'd called the White House "the Great White Prison." I suspect that the Blair House became something more of a prison for him after the violence outside.

I seldom saw Truman's daughter, Margaret, during my days at Blair House, even though Truman was extremely fond of her. He was also very protective of her. Sometimes, much to her embarrassment, he called her "Baby." In those days Margaret was spending most of her time in New York trying to advance a career as a singer. She was studying with Helen Traubel, the great American opera soprano well known for her Wagnerian roles. Traubel often performed with the Danish (later American) opera tenor, Lauritz Melchior.

Margaret was a pleasant person and singer, but not what you'd call a first-class artist. After she came to Washington to sing at the 3,800-seat Constitution Hall, the *Post's* chief critic, Paul Hume, panned the performance. I knew Paul, and even wrote music reviews for him for a while. He was a very touchy and stringy personality. He was determined, president's daughter or not, to criticize her the way he would anybody.

Truman could have a quick temper, especially when engaged in public matters, and more especially, with anything involving criticism of his daughter. When he felt angry about a public attack on himself or his policies as president, he'd usually blow off steam by writing an angry letter to the culprit. Then he'd never mail it. It's a policy that many would do well to consider in these days of e-mail and instant communications.

In Margaret's case, however, he not only wrote the letter—and a very angry one it was. He pulled out a little packet of stamps from his pocket, stamped the letter, walked down the street to the mailbox, and mailed it. "I have just read your lousy review buried in the back pages," the letter said. "You sound like a frustrated old man who never made a success, an eight-ulcer man on a four-ulcer job and all four ulcers working.

"I never met you, but if I do, you'll need a new nose and a supporter below. Westbrook Pegler, a guttersnipe, is a gentleman compared to you. You can take that as more of an insult than a reflection on your ancestry."

Twenty-five years later, at the National Press Club, journalists still chuckled a little nervously about that letter. But Paul Hume and the president made their peace before each man died, at least. Hume even made a friendly visit to Truman at his presidential library in Independence.

Of the others I saw while I played at the Blair House, I particularly remember Tom Clark, U.S. attorney general and later a justice of the U.S. Supreme Court. He always had a smile and a few words for me.

Truman had never wanted to be president. He'd reached that position almost accidentally, as a surprise choice for vice president, and then as an unelected president after Roosevelt's death. I'm sure that by the end of his second term in office, he was ready to move on. The last time I played for him, in 1952, he came up to me after I'd finished.

"Well, I guess we're both out of a job," he said, flashing his famous smile and offering me his hand.

I guess we were. But he'd left me with one of the most memorable impressions of my life, and plenty of plans for the future.

Ifor Jones
January 23, 1900 - November 11, 1988

William Ifor Jones, friend, musician, and mentor.
(Collection of George Manos)

President Truman leaves for the *U.S.S. Williamsburg* after a visit to the U.S. Naval Academy in 1948. (Truman Library)

The *Williamsburg* under way in 1948. (Truman Library)

President Truman (center, shirtless) on board the *Williamsburg* during a swim break off Blakiston Island in August 1948. (Truman Library)

President Truman poses in the *Williamsburg's* main saloon, the scene of much piano playing during lunch and dinner. (Truman Library)

Even after he left the presidency, President Truman continued to play and enjoy music. Here, he accompanies Jack Benny in September 1959, when Benny visited the Truman Library in Independence, Missouri, to give his television audience a tour of the just-opened facility.
(Truman Library)

The gifted baritone Todd Duncan: the first Porgy in *Porgy and Bess* and the first black performer to join the New York City Opera. He was friend, musical colleague, and inspiration. (Collection of George Manos)

The soprano Elena Nikolaidi, frequent companion on cross-country
musical tours and a fellow lover of Greek food.
(Collection of George Manos)

The Killarney Bach Festival celebrated its tenth anniversary with an homage to its namesake on its program's cover.
(Collection of George Manos)

George Manos in 1980. (Collection of George Manos)

5

Out of a Job

Truman's parting remark to me as he stepped down from the presidency was typical of his good-natured humor. We were both out of a job. But we both had plenty to do after the thirty-third president left office and power was transferred on Inauguration Day to Gen. Dwight D. Eisenhower. I had already been lining up extracurricular musical activities even while I was in the Marine Band. After I left, I kept my career going in several directions, as a pianist, conductor, teacher, and composer.

For his part, Truman kept busy back home in Independence writing his memoirs and creating the Harry S. Truman Presidential Library and Museum. He worked in the Federal Reserve Bank Building in Kansas City until 1957, when he moved his office to the newly completed Truman Library. That same year, he became a grandfather when Margaret bore her first son, Clifton Truman Daniel, named for his grandfather and for his father, Clifton Daniel, managing editor of *The New York Times.*

Truman and I traded letters a few times. I'd ask him to help me with a problem. His reply would invariably be that his involvement would likely create more problems than it would solve. His participation in government for so many years had taught him much about the bureaucratic process, and the limitations even of a president's power.

When Truman came back to visit Washington, he'd stay in the Presidential Suite in the apartments behind the Mayflower Hotel. Sometimes when Truman was in town, his aide (and my neighbor) David Stowe would call me and say, "The Boss is back in town and wants to see you."

I was only too glad to oblige, because Truman had become like another father to me. He was always full of kind words and gentle advice. Truman's biographers have said that he never forgot a friend, and that was true in my case. He was thoughtful enough when he returned to Washington to look me up.

When I visited Truman at the Mayflower, he'd offer me a jigger of whisky. He loathed bourbon himself, but he always took a shot in the morning. It seemed to get the system going, he said. I later learned that in his case, it really did. He had low blood pressure, and alcohol helped raise it to the proper level. His physician, Gen. Graham, had advised him to have a drink every day. To many of us, such doctor's orders would be easy to follow. But for Truman, they were probably difficult to swallow. When Truman was eight years old, he and his brother, Vivian, had both contracted diphtheria. The standard treatment in those days was bourbon and ipecac, a medical course of action meant to make the patient vomit the disease out of the system. Thus it was with little pleasure that Truman took his morning shot every day, although I suspect that many of his aides enjoyed the ritual well enough.

On my last visit to Truman at the Mayflower, I was ushered in past a group of five or six congressmen and senators waiting in the hall. One of them was Owen Brewster, a vocal Republican senator from Maine and a longtime nemesis of Truman's. As I passed, the politicians looked at me as if they were thinking, "Who is this young punk?" I was still just in my 20s.

Truman's apartment, which was on the fifth floor, overlooked 17th Street. It had its own private entrance and exit. When I knocked on the door, Gen. Vaughan opened it and said, in his gruff way, "Come in!"

It was about 10 in the morning. There was the president walking up to me and offering me a glass of whisky, his customary libation, which I politely declined. I have never been a morning drinker. He was surrounded by a number of aides besides Gen. Vaughan: David Stowe, my neighbor; George Mckee Elsey, the president's former administrative assistant; John R. Steelman, who by this time owned a number of weekly newspapers; and Gen. Graham. Gen. Graham was married to Ilona Massey, a beautiful movie star. I met her only once, years later, after Truman's death, on the night we dedicated the Truman Lounge at the National Press Club. Although I didn't know it, she had arthritis and a terrible hand problem. In those days, I had a very strong grip. When we greeted one another, she screamed bloody murder after I squeezed her hand. Hereafter, I suggested, when you want to shake hands with someone, give them your left hand. Later on, she and Gen. Graham divorced.

In his suite, Truman and I chatted about our careers for a while. Each of us was getting along well in our lives. Then the conversation somehow got around to Gen. Rubén Fulgencio Batista y Zaldivar. The corrupt Cuban president had left office during World War II but had regained the Cuban presidency through rigged elections. Truman had wanted to get him out. In those days, the world looked upon the insurgent Fidel Castro as the future George Washington of the island nation. Little did we realize our mistake: Far from being a savior of his country who would, like Washington, step down from office after liberating his compatriots, Castro turned out to be a Communist dictator who enslaved the country politically and ruined it economically. As usual, Truman talked brilliantly about history—Cuban and American, this time.

"I tried my best," Truman said. "I did the very best I could." As usual, his heart was with the underdog—in this case, the Cuban people.

Presently, an aide reminded Truman that he was scheduled to have lunch on the Hill. I tried to leave, but Truman said, "Stay and give me your arm. Walk down to the car with me." When I reminded him about his visitors awaiting him in the hallway, he said, "Those boys I can always see."

Some men seem to shrink after they leave positions of leadership, as if they had been puffed up by power and then deflated as if suddenly pricked by a pin. Not Truman. He still stood tall and walked at his customary brisk pace. This wasn't the case with all of his staff. Even the great Alonzo Fields, the tall, intelligent, and elegant butler who had smoothed over so many rough situations at the White House, seemed to diminish in size after he retired. But Truman still had his physical vitality and his great brain power, and the self-confidence of knowing who he was. The only change I noticed after his presidency was that he seemed even more relaxed and calm, now that the tremendous strain of the job had been lifted from him. But he still retained his military stature: shoulders back; head up; arms straight. I never got the impression that he was shriveling up. He was always on the go.

"Help me with my coat," he said. When we got to his limousine on the street, we exchanged farewells: "Good-bye. Be careful. Take care of yourself." Then he got in the limousine and sped off, accompanied by two cops on motorcycles. That was the last time I saw him in person. Every time I recall it, I think of his parting words: "I tried my best."

I never saw Harry Truman again after our last meeting at the Mayflower Hotel in Washington. As a struggling and striving musician, I was too poor, and then too busy, to get out to Missouri. When Truman died on December 26, 1972, I learned about it as others did—through TV, radio, and newspapers.

From the first time I met him until the end, he never really changed. His attitude didn't change. His ego didn't change. He had a wonderful sense of humor, and kept it throughout his years in one of the most difficult offices there is. He enjoyed the finer things in life, like great literature and great music. But he was completely unfazed by money and power and all the luxuries they could bring. He continued to drive his unspectacular Chrysler automobile after the presidency. He left the White House with the same suitcases he'd brought there. His luggage was the kind you could buy at any department store in those days. The suitcases had a phony leather veneer that had been blackish-brown at one time, but they'd turned a sort of reddish-clay color when the veneer had worn off and revealed the underlying cardboard.

One day shortly after Truman had left office, I asked his aide and my neighbor David Stowe what the president would do now. Then it occurred to me that he could have easily become a college professor. Stowe agreed. You could mention any period in the history of the human race, and Truman would tell you all about it. His love of reading good history and biography and his sharp mind remained with him for the rest of his life.

I've often wondered if the United States would be in so many predicaments if Truman were still around. He had not only an amazing knowledge of history and an extraordinarily perceptive take on current events. He also knew how to surround himself with sharp men like Clark Clifford, his special advisor, and Dean Acheson, his secretary of state.

Truman faced some of the greatest crises of the 20th century, and steered the United States and the world through them all. He guided us through the end of World War II. He used the atomic bomb, reluctantly but willingly, to end the war with Japan after giving the Japanese fair warning that they faced annihilation. His Marshall Plan helped our former enemies recover after the end of World War II, and may have prevented another world war. He even dispatched an old political foe and former president, Herbert Hoover, to Europe to help relieve starvation there after the war.

The Korean War was far from a success, but Truman at least managed to keep us out of a third world war as animosities with China and the Soviet Union grew. He initiated the Central Intelligence Agency, it is true. But it was only under future presidents and directors that its mission to collect and centralize intelligence was perverted to domestic spying and cloak-and-dagger escapades overseas.

Every president bears an immense burden, as photographs show through the wrinkles and gray hairs acquired by presidents during their tenure. Truman acquitted himself more than well in office. I'd even venture to predict that someday he'll go down in history as the greatest president of the 20th century. He certainly was the most underrated. That underestimation has much to do, curiously, with one of his finer qualities: his modesty, and lack of pretense and self-promotion.

As a student of history, Truman was fond of observing that each generation ignores the lessons of history, and has to learn the hard way, through bitter experience, on its own. Such was the case with his successors in office. He could have been a help to later presidents. Unfortunately, he was ignored. That policy started with his immediate successor, Dwight D. Eisenhower, who snubbed Truman at his inauguration in 1953. It continued, though in a less hostile manner, down to the day of Truman's death.

Some of Eisenhower's successors paid Truman token respect, at least. John F. Kennedy invited Truman to his inauguration in January 1961, and later, in November, to dinner at the White House, where Eugene List entertained the diners with a piano concert of music by Chopin and Mozart. List even asked Truman to play for a while, which he did. I'm sure that he played with his usual gusto, good humor, and love of music.

6

Prelude to a Career

I was out of a job, as Truman had said, but I made my own way in the musical world. When many of us think of classical music, we recall great geniuses like Beethoven and Mozart, who suffered for their art and met tragic fates. Fortunately, a good classical musician was able to make a decent living in the 20th century in the United States.

Some, like Aaron Copland and Leonard Bernstein, earned a very good living indeed. Others have made fortunes off their musical kin's labors. I think of this particularly when I recall the great Russian composer Dmitri Shostakovich, whose son I met one day years ago at my brother's car dealership in Maryland.

I'd gone in to buy a car from my brother. When I went into his office, he said, "I want you to meet someone who's here." It turned out to be Shostakovich's son, Maksim. I was delighted to meet him, because I adored his father's music.

When I met the younger Shostakovich, it was plain that he knew English. But he wouldn't speak to me. There was a KGB man with him who spoke perfect English. He handled all the talking. The KGB man said that he was with the press out of the Soviet embassy, but I knew better. These were ripe times to defect. I spoke to Shostakovich's son as best I could through this interpreter, but we didn't get very far.

The next time Maksim returned to the United States, it was with his wife, which the Soviet Union hadn't allowed before, fearing that they would defect together. But gradually things began to loosen up as relations improved between the United States and the Soviet Union. When Shostakovich finally could move to the United States, he became a multimillionaire overnight.

We have strict international copyrights in this country. Anyone who'd performed a piece by Dmitri Shostakovich had to pay a fee. These sums added up over the years. The composer's son got all of that when he emigrated to the United States. He himself worked as a pianist and conducted the New Orleans Symphony for a time, but he didn't have that much success. He wasn't as amazing a talent as his father. I imagine that his father's money took some of the sting out of his own musical limits. He ended up moving to Greenwich, Connecticut, and living in luxury.

Although I didn't wind up as wealthy as Bernstein, Copland, or Shostakovich's son, I made my way. It was a long, hard climb. But by the time I'd finished playing piano for Truman, my name had already become well known in Washington. My mentors Ifor Jones and Austin Conradi also helped me along. I advanced as a pianist, conductor, composer, teacher, and administrator, often doing several things at once.

In the summer of 1952, before Truman had left office, I'd helped Leonard Bernstein at the Tanglewood Music Festival in the beautiful Berkshire Mountains of Massachusetts. Tanglewood was my introduction to the big time in classical music. Hugh Ross, head of the vocal and choral department, had asked me to come up. He knew me through one of my mentors at the Peabody Conservatory, Ifor Jones. Ross was looking for a double threat: a good choral director and a good pianist. I helped him prepare Franz Joseph Haydn's *Theresien Mass*. And I helped Charles Münch, conductor of the Boston Symphony, prepare Berlioz' *Romeo and Juliet* and Brahms' *German Requiem*. That was enough. I worked my rear end off all summer at Tanglewood. Münch had taken over conducting of the Boston Symphony and Tanglewood after the Russian-born conductor and composer Serge Koussevitsky's death in 1951. Leonard Bernstein would have very much liked to have had those jobs. He had sailed along on Koussevitsky's coattails, no matter where he went. He was Koussevitsky's boy.

Münch was in many ways the stereotypical Frenchman: emotional, florid, and a bon vivant. Like many musicians who came to Tanglewood, he seemed to regard it as a sort of summer camp for adults. He was quite a drinker. Between movements during rehearsals, he always helped himself to a martini. He must have been in his 60s when I worked under him, but was an impressive presence. He was fairly tall, an inch or two under six feet, and had a full head of gray hair. Despite his drinking, he was still very sharp and thorough during rehearsals.

I worked with his chorus on *Romeo and Juliet* and the *German Requiem*. He used to treat me like an orchestra, having me play everything on the piano. We'd be up there on stage, and I was all over the place on the piano. I had ten hands all the time, because those are two very big works to play just on piano. He'd conduct me with his stick, and sometimes he'd try to catch me off guard, just to see if I were awake. But I wouldn't allow it. I kept up with him. He'd turn back to the chorus with a wink. And he'd shout at the singers. He was working with a bunch of Americans who were singing in his native language, French, and in German, in which he was also fluent. It must have been very frustrating for him to listen to them mangle the tongues.

They had no facilities for me at Tanglewood, so I stayed at a private residence in Lenox. Every morning at eight, I'd go in to rehearse. Because I had no car, I'd start walking down the highway toward the Tanglewood grounds. Invariably someone would stop and ask me if I were going to Tanglewood. I'd say yes, hop in the car, and get there soon. Same thing going home. I can't imagine that happening these days.

Musicians from all over the world came to Tanglewood. Some were established; some were trying to get noticed. My mentor Ifor Jones was there. He was the choral man, and a standby orchestral man. Years earlier he'd worked at Tanglewood with the amazing singer Mario Lanza. The Philadelphia-born Lanza had an incredible voice, but practically no formal musical training. Serge Koussevitsky, who was head man at Tanglewood and the Boston Symphony then, had Lanza sing for him. The great conductor and composer was thrilled with Lanza's powerful voice, and went absolutely bananas after he heard him. But when he found out that Lanza had no formal grounding in music, he palmed him off on Jones.

Ifor Jones tried to teach Lanza basic music theory. Like a strict schoolmaster, he drilled Lanza every day.

"This is a piece of music and it has 4:4 rhythm," Jones would say.

"What do you mean by that?" Lanza would ask.

"Oh, God," Jones would say to himself, and moan inwardly. He'd explain that there were four beats to a bar. "The other four means quarter note," Jones would go on. "The quarter note means that you have one, two, three, four."

Lanza nodded his head.

"Try to read me the first few bars," Jones said, encouraged.

So Lanza began: "One, two, three, four, five, six, seven…."

Jones broke in: "If you continue on, you'll be up in the millions!"

Poor Lanza flunked out of Tanglewood, as far as Jones was concerned, but that didn't stop him from enjoying immense success in Hollywood and in opera. His singing career was cut short by a fatal heart attack in 1959, however. He was only 37 years old.

The singers I worked with at Tanglewood were almost like a student body. They came to sing and have fun. But they were very serious about their singing. When I was rehearsing the choir, I didn't have to worry much about wrong notes or training. They could sight read as well as I.

At Tanglewood, I also got to meet and work with illustrious musicians like Aaron Copland and Leonard Bernstein. Copland and I had a mutual friend, Katharine Hansel, a world-class soprano in Washington whom I'd started to accompany on piano in and around the city. By then Copland was getting along in age. He'd accompanied Hansel when she performed some of his pieces in New England. Some years later we finally got Copland to agree to come to the Peabody Conservatory in Baltimore, where he and Hansel performed some of the Emily Dickinson poems that Copland had set to music.

Copland's work was very difficult, although not what I'd call quite left field—or what my mentor Austin Conradi used to bitterly call contemporary classical music: "contemptuous" music. Copland's music was easily listened to and enjoyed. And, of course, Dickinson's poetry is wonderful. It's beautiful stuff, with a lot of humor. You're bound to get a good reaction from an audience when you sing a line like, "Why did they shut me out of heaven, did I sing too loud?" The only weak part of the performance was that, as I say, Copland was getting a little old, and his piano playing could have been better.

At Tanglewood, Bernstein, of course, had been the apple of conductor Koussevitsky's eye. You had to give Bernstein credit. He was brilliant. He was a great accompanist. He could play jazz on the piano, or classical. He wrote music like a fiend. And he knew everybody. He had that Harvard say-so. I've never known a Harvard man who was slow on vocabulary or verbiage. But I always also had the feeling that when Bernstein was talking to me at Tanglewood, he was looking out of the corner of his eye to see if any important visitors were coming onto the scene, so he could run over and latch onto them.

I suppose that my poor opinion of Bernstein is colored in part by his awful treatment of Dimitri Mitropoulos, a Greek-born conductor, pianist, and composer who was a genius. Mitropoulos was a conductor of the New York Philharmonic Symphony Orchestra from 1951 to 1957. I'd seen him before when he'd come down to Washington to guest-conduct the National Symphony. He was a phenomenal talent. He could conduct a Mahler symphony without a score. During rehearsals, he'd stop us, look at the six horn players, and say something like, "Third horn, page 368, bar 322. The fourth note is flat." He meant it. And he was always right.

Mitropoulos lived in a tiny apartment in New York with religious icons on the walls. These were left over from his college days, when he'd started out to become a priest. Priest or no, he remained very spiritual about things later in life. He explained to me once that he had no family, no hobbies, and nothing to do but study scores in his spare time. Which he did, memorizing them perfectly.

Mitropoulos was notorious for selecting and conducting ultra-modern music. It was worse than left field. It was out of the park. Crazy things by Ernst Krenek, the Austrian-born composer given to jazz opera and weirder music that none of us could follow.

Bernstein had badly wanted to conduct the Boston Symphony, as I've mentioned, but Koussevitsky had given the post to the Frenchman Münch, who did very well with it. Bernstein was devastated. He began working his contacts in New York. I knew that Mitropoulos wouldn't last long at the New York Philharmonic, which was notorious for high turnover among its conductors. He was so easy-going that they walked all over him. And now Bernstein was on the prowl.

Bernstein finally landed the position at the New York Philharmonic, though nobody bothered to tell Mitropoulos. One day I was at a rehearsal in New York with Mitropoulos and Elena Nikolaidi, a Greek opera singer who was one of his favorites. She used to do Mahler works like *Song of the Earth* with him. She and I were sitting in the orchestra during rehearsal. When it came time for intermission, Bernstein tripped up onstage to see the conductor.

"I've just been appointed," he exclaimed to Mitropoulos, "to take your job!"

We thought that really stunk, of course. I didn't quite hear what Mitropoulos said. I have a pretty good idea, though. It was in Greek.

Bernstein took a piece of paper out of his pocket, showed it to Mitropoulos, and said, "Look here. I begin next month, after you leave."

"But I want you to know that you're welcome to come back and guest-conduct any time," Bernstein added.

At that point, Nikolaidi let out a loud guffaw. She thought this was absolutely hideous, as did I. She issued a number of loud words in Greek, which I won't translate.

Such were the ups and downs of a pleasant summer at Tanglewood and beyond. I graduated from the Peabody Conservatory that same year of 1952. Technically, I got my degree from Johns Hopkins University, the Peabody's mother institution. I still receive letters from that university dunning me for alumni contributions.

7

Adventures in Music

Out of school, I continued to make music, sometimes for fun, sometimes for profit, often for both.

I performed as a pianist at the National Gallery of Art and the Phillips Museum in Washington. I played at Constitution Hall for the National Symphony. Hans Kindler, the founder of the orchestra and a world-class cellist—the same man who had treated me so well when I was just a kid trying to learn about music—had turned the orchestra over to his principal cellist, Howard Mitchell, in 1950.

Mitchell had never conducted a major orchestra before in his life, and he had a hell of a time with the job. It seldom pays for someone to come up through the ranks and conduct. The rest of the orchestra suffers from envy, and such a conductor can almost always read the question in their faces: "Who the hell do you think you are now?"

Mitchell was a wonderful cellist, but his troubles as a conductor were compounded by his terrible temper. At first, I couldn't find his beats. And if a member of his orchestra couldn't find his beats, he'd glare at you. But I caught on finally and became the National Symphony's chief pianist. The way I learned to follow Mitchell was to bring the entire orchestral score to rehearsals, rather than just the piano music. That way, I could keep up and know exactly where the conductor was all the time. Some of the other musicians saw my method and asked for help.

They'd say to me, "When you get to five bars, give us a nod. Because we never know, Howard never gives us a cue, and we have a hell of a time finding our spot." So I ended up giving a lot of Mitchell's cues to the orchestra with subtle nods of my head. Clueless musicians would look at me very closely as their point of entry approached, and then I'd give them the sign. It saved a lot of arguments.

Even so, Mitchell would often stop the rehearsals to give hell to a hapless fellow in the back on the string bass, cowering behind me and my piano.

"Now look at that guy! Look at Manos!" the maestro would shout. "I don't have trouble with him at all. He's always on cue." He thought I was marvelous because I didn't give him any problems.

I kept busy in other ways. I founded three oratorio societies in the 1950s—the Hellenic, Washington, and National—and conducted them until 1967. We performed music of the 18th through the 20th centuries, and gave the first performances of the French composer Maurice Duruflé's *Requiem* and the American composer Alan Hovhaness' *Magnificat*. As founder of the societies, I also shouldered much of the administrative burden: appointing legal counsel, fundraising, and conducting the day-to-day business of the organizations. It took a lot of effort because I had to deal with boards who were ignorant—probably just as ignorant as I. I never got paid for starting and running these societies.

I did get a plum position as organist and choir director for the National Presbyterian Church in Washington, which helped my financial situation greatly. The congregation had lots of money, and I worked there for ten years. Thanks to the oratorio societies, I'd already built a reputation as a choir director. There were concerts at the church throughout the year that included orchestra, for which I used members of the National Symphony. I had a 42-member chorus and we'd perform a Bach cantata every Sunday.

Shortly before President Kennedy's assassination, I'd been rehearsing my choir to perform Duruflé's new *Requiem*. I'd fallen in love with that piece after hearing a recording of Duruflé himself performing it with a Parisian group. Nobody else wanted to try it.

After JFK's death, I wondered if I should cancel the performance. The Catholic cathedral where they held the Kennedy Mass, St. Matthew's, was just around the corner, after all, and it might be considered unseemly. I called up my old friend Paul Hume, the *Post's* chief music critic and Truman's one-time nemesis after he'd panned Margaret Truman's performance at Constitution Hall.

"Don't you dare cancel," Hume said. "People are going to be upset. What a wonderful place to come, whether Catholic or Protestant. You're doing a beautiful, brand-new piece of work, and I can guarantee you you're going to be packed. There are going to be people who will be turned away."

He was right. The bells in the tower tolled all day long, and all night too. We had visitors who wanted to get out rather than stay at home. A lot of people feel better when they go to church and listen to a good sermon or good music.

The Duruflé *Requiem* would have been a half-hour short for a full program, so we performed a work by Handel also. The performance was marvelous: dignified yet comforting. The French composer's works were performed regularly in Washington thereafter.

At the National Symphony, I played under guest conductors like Leonard Bernstein, Leopold Stokowski, Sir Thomas Beecham, and other world-class talents. I got to work with Stokowksi, who had once been a fellow student with my mentor Ifor Jones, more closely when he came to Washington in 1955 to conduct a Mozart Festival at the Library of Congress. To me, Stokowski was frightening. He had that reputation. He was the great man, and a myth long before I met him. His shock of white hair, his stern face, his deliberate movements made him an imposing figure, and he took advantage of all that. Though, really, Toscanini was far more temperamental and tyrannical. Stokowksi was all about show business. But he had a great mind.

I'd been hired as the organist for the Mozart Festival. One day, after rehearsing the music that we were going to do for the chorus, I went home. When I returned for rehearsal the next morning, I caught hell from Stokowski.

"Mr. Organist!" he bawled. He never called any musician by name.

"Yes, maestro?" I said timidly.

"I looked for you yesterday."

"Well," I said, "we finished."

"Nothing is finished," he said grandly, "until the conductor leaves."

I had to admit that he was right. And he could have chewed me out much more thoroughly if he'd wished.

I also worked with the famed composer Igor Stravinsky when he came to Washington to conduct the National Symphony. It was a concert of his own music: *Petrouchka, Le Sacre du Printemps*, and *Firebird*.

During one of his rehearsals, this little man called the entire orchestra back to his dressing room, which was no bigger than a small living room. Picture 85 or 90 men crowding into this small space! Stravinsky had a towel wrapped around his head. He was puffing a cigarette. All he said was, "Gentlemen, the *Petrouchka* is very difficult. *Le Sacre du Printemps* is very difficult. *Firebird* is very difficult." In one hand, he held a jigger of brandy. Then he said, "That's all! Thank you!" We all walked out scratching our heads.

Stravinksy was a real conductor, though, and another example of a classical musician who made a good living as a composer and conductor. He earned every penny of it. Some have called him the greatest composer of the 20th century. He opened up new doors of harmonic and contrapuntal writing. A lot of his music became a staple in the United States. Just about every orchestra performed it.

As a result, many younger composers wanted to study with him. But he refused to teach anyone. Of course, Stravinsky had worked with one of the greatest musical pedagogues the world has ever known: Nikolai Rimsky-Korsakov, who wrote countless opera and symphonies and whose book on orchestration became the handbook of teachers and composers around the world. Stravinksy had benefited hugely from his mentor. But Stravinsky simply didn't teach. He was easy to work with as a conductor, though.

During these years I also earned a good living and had a marvelous time as a piano accompanist for three great singers: Katharine Hansel, Elena Nikolaidi, and Todd Duncan. We'd play in Washington at smaller locations, and at bigger places like Constitution Hall. We'd also go on the road. Hansel limited her road trips to nearby places because she didn't want to stray too far from her four children at home. Duncan, because he was black, normally stayed north of the Mason-Dixon Line due to the South's lingering racial prejudice. Nikolaidi and I ranged across the wide expanses of the United States and Canada.

My association with Hansel lasted 20 years. She was a world-class soprano who lived in Washington. Because of her four daughters, we'd perform mainly in town, in smaller places like the National Gallery's garden courts or the Phillips Collection. We must have performed at those sites 40 or 50 times.

Katharine Hansel was a red-headed beauty and a great dresser. Her gorgeous gowns added to her stage presence, as did her command of the material. The latter came from hard effort. She worked as much or more than anyone I knew. When she walked onto the stage, she almost could say that she'd composed the music that she would sing. She knew it that well. That's why composers like Copland liked her so much. He knew that she'd perform difficult pieces of his as if she'd written them herself.

When I accompanied her, she performed a tremendous variety of vocal repertoire. She was a great singer, and could handle anything: German Lieder; French art songs; American songs by composers like Copland. She gave many first performances of my own compositions, often of Greek poetry set to music.

Elena Nikolaidi sang many of my Greek songs too. She was Greek, like me, which may be part of the reason we got along so well. We often chatted in Greek, and she shared my love of Greek food and music. She sang the Greek songs that I'd written with special gusto.

Nikolaidi was a mezzo-soprano who came from the Vienna State Opera. She was highly respected in Austria and throughout Europe. Her admirers included conductors like Arturo Toscanini and Bruno Walter. In the United States, she sang with the Metropolitan Opera. I met her and we hit it off. She had a studio at the Ansonia Hotel in New York, and I'd often go there to rehearse with her. My sister Helen lived in New York then, and I'd stay with her or with Nikolaidi.

Columbia Artists Management in New York signed Nikolaidi and me to go on tour. Our travels ranged across the country, through the South and out West, up North and into Canada. We'd perform what in those days was called *Lieder abend*, a night of song. Nikolaidi would sing German Lieder and French art songs, accompanied by me at the piano, of course. As a Greek, she particularly loved to sing the Greek songs that I'd composed.

Our first big tour for Columbia Artists started in Winter Park, Florida, continued to Tampa, then to Selma, Alabama, and out to Texas, where we spent a month playing at small towns like Nacogdoches and in bigger cities like Houston. Then we went up to Oklahoma, where oil money could fund cultural endeavors such as ours. I still remember seeing a 20-story skyscraper rising out of the flat Oklahoma landscape at Bartlesville. It had been designed and built by Frank Lloyd Wright. It was a beautiful building, but it stuck out like a sore thumb in that rather bleak country.

Nikolaidi and I had one big complaint about Columbia. Although the company sent us everywhere, it cut corners on transportation costs. In fact, we felt like a couple of hobos. Nikolaidi dressed in minks and gowns, and I wore my formal concert attire. We both carried beautiful luggage. To have to travel by bus was humiliating. It was, and remains, the lowest form of travel. We felt very out of place crammed in with the poor rustics on the buses as we made our way around the country.

We also learned during our tours that many smaller Southern towns seemed to close up after six. Getting something decent to eat for dinner became a problem. When we'd get into a town, we'd call on the concert hall and check to see if the piano and acoustics were OK, and if the floor was clean. (By the end of our tours, Nikolaidi's very expensive gowns would be black on the bottoms from all the dirt and dust.) By the time we got to our hotel, we'd often find that no restaurant was still open where we could have dinner. So we subsisted on peanut-butter crackers and Cokes and Orangeade we bought from vending machines in hotel lobbies.

We did find occasional respite, thanks to Nikolaidi's initiative. After a performance at Nacogdoches, Texas, she turned to me and said, in Greek, "Come over here, George, there's country here." Meaning that a couple of Greek-Americans had come backstage knowing that Nikolaidi and I were both Greek-Americans also.

"We hope you don't mind," our visitors said, "but we brought you some goodies." They gave us two big boxes. One held a cake. The other had leg of lamb, Greek-style potatoes, feta cheese, and other Greek delicacies. Nikolaidi and I thanked our guests profusely, brought the boxes back to our hotel, and ate like pigs.

At Oklahoma City, a wealthy woman came backstage after the performance and wanted to know all about us. She asked Nikolaidi when she would sing again at the Met. Somehow Nikolaidi steered the conversation around to the subject of Greek food. After a while, Nikolaidi cast a sidelong glance at me as she said to her rich admirer, "Oh, I will cook for you!"

We stayed in Oklahoma for two and a half days. The wealthy lady sent her limousine and chauffeur over to our hotel the next day to pick us up and to take us shopping. When we got to our hostess's house, a sprawling ranch, we cooked up a Greek storm: moussaka, pastichio, eggplant, and loads of other Greek goodies. We must have spent four or five hours preparing the meal. This lady invited 25 friends to her mansion, and we all feasted like Greek gods and goddesses. We made plenty for all. In fact, Nikolaidi made sure to cook more than enough. The leftovers we took from that dinner nourished us in town for the next few days, and on the plane ride back to New York.

Our most grueling trip was to the North Bay country in Canada. I was back in Washington, and Nikolaidi in New York. We'd agreed to meet in Canada. I flew to Toronto from Washington, rented a car, and began driving north resolutely through a blinding snowstorm. Finally, I had to stop. I could go no farther, and I pulled into a service station. A man came out and said, "Do you know where you are?"

I said, "No, but I'm headed for North Bay."

"It's down the road," he said, "but you'll never make it in this weather. Mister, I can take you there." Which he did. (He also later returned my rental car to the airport.)

After what seemed like days of driving, or perhaps flying, so difficult was it to see, we found the concert hall. I thanked the driver, paid him, and walked inside the building—just in time for the post-concert reception. We all had a marvelous laugh, followed by a good dinner and a flight back to New York the next day.

I worked with Nikolaidi until years later she joined the faculty at Florida State University in Tallahassee. Later still, she taught in Houston.

My travels with Todd Duncan, the world-famous baritone, were much more limited due to the racial prejudice that still lingered in parts of the country in those days. We would only perform above the Mason-Dixon Line and in places in the South where blacks were allowed to attend performances.

Duncan was a king—an artist. He was getting older when I worked with him, but he was still a powerful singer, and a genius. He spoke four languages. His French and German were impeccable. He sang German Lieder, French art songs, and American spirituals, all magnificently. I was his third and last accompanist.

George Gershwin had watched Duncan sing, and picked him to be the first man to play Porgy in his historic opera *Porgy and Bess*. I could see why. Duncan was an artist of the first rank. You could tell where his powerful voice came from. He was a bull of a man who stood about six foot one. He looked like a fullback. He combined his imposing physique with a sharp and creative mind to create some of the greatest music of his day. After a while, people didn't see black, white, or color at all. They just saw great artistry.

Duncan had a magnificent home in Washington, at 16th and F streets, not far from where I lived. He'd done very well financially as a performer and also as an immensely popular teacher. When he came to Washington with his wife, Gladys, to play Porgy in *Porgy and Bess* at the National Theater, the first thing he did was to say that he'd perform there only if blacks were allowed to attend and to sit wherever they wanted. That created quite a stir. Management finally yielded, much to the benefit of its reputation in the long term. Duncan's wife had a lot to do with it. She was one of those women who would sit down at lunch counters, even in those early days, and wait until she got served.

Once down in Virginia or the Carolinas, I forget which, we appeared at a posh finishing school for young black ladies. Their beautiful attire included elegant white gloves.

Duncan stopped after singing a few songs and in his booming voice said, "Are you enjoying my music?"

The crowd applauded and cried out yes.

"I can't hear you!" Duncan said. "Take off those gloves."

They did, and began shouting and clapping wildly, much to Duncan's pleasure.

He was a great artist to work with. His was a brilliant genius mind, vocally and culturally. People like Duncan had reputations as dragons. Not with me. I loved to accompany him. And I learned a lot from him about singing, which helped me with my choral work. I'd often sit in on the singing lessons he gave. I'd just stay in a corner and listen as he worked with his students. That's where I learned how to work with singers, and to teach them to open up their larynxes.

Sometimes Duncan would ask me to play the piano to accompany a student. Once, I remember, I accompanied one who was going to sing a piece by Mendelssohn.

Right before the singer took a breath, Duncan cried, "Stop! I'm not going to like it!"

"I haven't made a sound," the student protested.

"That's the point," Duncan replied. "I can see it in your face. Besides, you took a breath like Manos would take a breath."

The student tried to start again.

"That's wrong," Duncan said. "You have to learn to soak in the air. Use the diaphragm."

I got a voice lesson every time I watched Duncan teach a pupil, and also at each of our rehearsals. I'd go to Duncan's house almost every day at 10 or 10:30 in the morning. Duncan would start singing. It was a bit like listening to a powerful old steam engine coming to life. I'd say, "You know, you sound a bit rough."

He'd reply, "You just wait." Within a half-hour, he'd have rid himself of all the extraneous garbage in his voice—the one he woke up with. He knew what to do, where to go, how to breathe, and how to place the voice properly.

Every moment I had with these superb singers—Duncan, Nikolaidi, and Hansel—was not only a job, but a lesson. So it was also with my teaching, where I learned as much as I taught. I added academics to my other responsibilities when I began teaching at American University in Washington in 1962. Four years later I accepted a position at Washington's Catholic University. A colleague, Emerson Myers, had studied under my mentor Austin Conradi 20 or so years before I had. Myers had become a first-rate concert pianist. He'd spend summers in Liege, in Belgium, teaching and giving piano recitals. In 1962, he decided to spend a whole year in Belgium, and I replaced him temporarily at Catholic University.

I taught piano literature: the music of Bach, Beethoven, Brahms, Mozart, Chopin, and on down the list. I had a studio with two Steinway concert grands. I'd sit at one; my student would sit at the other. We'd discuss the literature. I'd play for the students. They'd play for me. I had a wonderful time with the graduate students at Catholic University.

When Myers returned, we started a doctor of musical arts degree program at the university. There weren't many candidates. Maybe four or five. But they worked their tails off. During the two-year program, they'd give four or five recitals. A lot of the music was contemporary and very brainy. You'd have to learn the American contemporary composer George Rochberg's famous and horribly difficult *Sonata*, take it to bed with you, and have nightmares about it.

Fortunately, our graduate students were very bright and skilled at playing the piano. One night when Myers and I were having dinner, he looked at me and said, "You know, George, if you and I had to go through this program, I doubt if we'd pass it." I had to agree with him. I was delighted we didn't have to do the coursework that we were assigning our students.

The undergraduates were another matter. I flunked many of them. Few seemed willing to put in the long hours of practice needed to master the piano. Occasionally they protested with what seemed to be amazing naïveté.

"Professor Manos, do you realize that you flunked us?" said one of two bright young girls who came into my office together one day.

"Yes," I said. "Do you want to know why?"

"Well, we haven't really practiced that hard," she conceded.

"No, you haven't," I said. "You come to an hour lesson and you give ten minutes' worth of work. The other 50 minutes you run out when you should be practicing. You're wasting your time and mine."

One boy was bolder. A few days after I told him that he needed to shape up, he brought his mother to complain. I said the same thing to his mother.

"Your little James here gave me ten minutes' worth of study. He hasn't gone past the first page," I said. "What am I going to do with this kid?"

Little James calmed down and never came back, with or without his mother. My philosophy was that I had enough experience and knowledge that I wasn't going to pull my students' socks up for them. Now that I look back, it seems that it may have been the beginning of a narcissistic phase in American history, where practically all students began to feel that they were geniuses and didn't need to study at all. Cultural and intellectual entitlement, if you will. You see the result now on such sad shows as *American Idol*: people with no talent and no training who produce nauseating music, get shot down, and fall to pieces.

I should have been prepared. I'd seen even more decadence, laziness, and smugness when I'd taught music at the Madeira School, a hoity-toity prep school for girls in the Virginia countryside. If the name's familiar, it may be because a future headmistress of the school, Jean Harris, gained notoriety many years later for slaying her unfaithful lover, Dr. Herman Tarnower, author of the best-selling weight-loss book *The Scarsdale Diet*.

These Madeira girls were so wealthy that they brought their horses to school with them every term. The school provided stables where they could board their steeds. At the beginning of the year, as we teachers waited expectantly, we'd see trucks coming down the road bearing the horses, and limousines pulling up and depositing these rich little darlings at their dormitories.

These were high-school kids, prone to rebellion anyway. In my first encounters with them, I was met with almost total indifference. The girls spent most of their class time chatting and gossiping. I told them, "I don't give a damn if your father is Mr. Swift of Swift Meats or what have you. I'm here to do a job. You're here to learn. And that's all there is to it."

I made little headway until the headmistress finally helped me, perhaps out of pity. One day, I got a mysterious call from her.

"George, the sheep are in the pasture. You know what that means, don't you?"

I did. I had dismissed the wild girls from the classroom and they were simply wandering about the lovely campus.

"Yeah," I said. "Gag the little bitches."

She offered to deny the girls passes for going out. That quickly brought about discipline. And it helped that the headmistress, rather than I, was punishing them. Once she'd helped steer the girls in line, I taught them all how to read music, how to sing, and how to sing in parts. They began enjoying it. I said, "Aren't you proud of yourselves?" Most of them were. Some were so rich that they didn't give a damn.

I broke up my seven years of teaching at Catholic University with a three-year stint as executive director of the Wilmington School of Music in Wilmington, Delaware. This was DuPont country, and the school was funded by DuPont money. Students of any age could study there. It was not a degree-granting institution. But I started a diploma course for those who wanted to go on to college.

The school had its own building and a beautiful auditorium. Given the copious amounts of DuPont money on hand, there were Steinways all over the place. It was a bit like working for the government, though. The school's governing board was full of members of the Du Pont family or people who worked for them. This was far from a blessing. Rather, it was often a bureaucratic nightmare. The family recently had run the DuPont corporation so incompetently that the company had been forced to import an executive from Minnesota to set things right.

In my last year at Wilmington, I was so sick of the stifling bureaucracy there that I was ready to quit. But the school asked me to stay to help celebrate its 50th anniversary. School officials placated me, temporarily, by putting me up in the Hotel du Pont in downtown Wilmington. It was a beautiful building staffed by employees who gave guests white-glove, European-style service. I'd take the train from my home in Bethesda to Wilmington, and spend three days a week at the du Pont. The school paid for my lodgings, transportation, and three meals a day, which I usually took in the hotel's elegant dining room.

I was unhappy at the Wilmington School of Music, but I did enjoy some success. I started a theory department and a jazz program. I liked jazz, and so did the students, it turned out. I'd get topnotch jazzmen like Herbie Hancock to come to the school and teach. We got some money from the local arts council and took the program to some of Delaware's public schools, where it also became a success.

A similar effort with classical music in Delaware didn't work as well, much to my dismay. I assembled an orchestra of about 45 pieces. I called an old friend, Ann Kocielny, a distinguished lady and an incredible pianist whom I'd worked with at the National Gallery and at other places in Washington. I convinced her to join us on a tour of Delaware's public schools, where we we'd present Mozart's *39th Symphony*.

The orchestra played beautifully as we made our way from one school to the next down the Delaware peninsula. At the last school, I made the mistake of looking over my shoulder after conducting. The audience barely applauded. I turned around to face my listeners.

"Did you enjoy it?" I asked the assembly of high-school students.

To a boy and a girl, they responded as with one voice, with a simple and resounding "No!" It was as if the unified response had been rehearsed.

I wrote the principal a nasty letter later. High-school kids today know life. There isn't a virgin in the class. But they don't understand the most beautiful things in life.

Of course, throughout the turbulent 1960s, I'd been busy with other things too. I continued to give piano recitals, often at the National Gallery and in Wilmington. For three years, I conducted the National Ballet of Washington. Once I took it on a tour of the United States and Mexico with Hugo Fiorato of the New York Ballet.

In 1964, I joined my mentor Ifor Jones in Bethlehem, Pennsylvania, as associate conductor of the Bethlehem Bach Festival. For many years, he'd been conductor of the foremost Bach festival in the land. Music lovers would come from all over the United States, Europe, and South America. You couldn't get a ticket to the festival unless one of the guarantors died. They used to pipe the performance music across the street to another auditorium where, for a small fee, you could go in and listen to an audio version. Or, if the weather was good, and the officials opened all the windows at Packer Chapel, you could bring a blanket and a picnic and listen outside.

I served as Ifor Jones' understudy conductor, to be on hand, I guess, in case he got sick or died. I learned a lot in Bethlehem, and met a lot of people too. Unfortunately, my tenure there came to an end after just three years.

As I've mentioned, Jones was an intelligent, good-looking man with a beautiful Welsh speaking and singing voice. He seemed to be going through some sort of male menopause during the time I assisted him in Bethlehem, however. He began to like and drive sports cars. A pretty young thing started making amorous overtures to him. This was nothing new to a handsome Welshman like Jones. But I guess at his age, he suddenly felt very spry again, having this young, good-looking gal playing up to him. She was a singer, although she didn't sing in the festival.

The only real problem was that Jones was married, to the distinguished English singer Lillian Knowles. His young lady friend made it quite evident that she was there, and of course Lillian didn't like it. It also didn't look good to the conservative powers that were at Bethlehem. The place was funded largely with money from Bethlehem Steel Corporation. Everyone loved and respected Lillian, and felt terrible about her husband's affair.

Jones took his adventures past the point of no return. He and his wife lived in a beautiful estate in Bethlehem, from which Jones would drive to Philadelphia and take the train to Baltimore to teach at the Peabody Conservatory. Lillian Knowles finally moved out and got herself a small house in the poor part of Bethlehem. Jones then moved in with his lady friend. The Bach Choir didn't like that at all. It didn't look good. Lillian gave Jones a divorce. He stayed on with the Bach Choir for another year or two and then resigned, after 33 years as conductor.

I was slated to become conductor after Jones stepped down. He was convinced that I would continue the level of excellence that he'd established in Bethlehem. Through some skullduggery, however, I wasn't chosen. It is a known fact that over the years since Jones departed, the festival has declined. It has never regained the world-class renown it had attained under Ifor Jones.

I'd always had a flair for the dramatic and for the spotlight, from the time I was a child and gave weekly radio recitals with my sister on WBIG in Greensboro, North Carolina. Years later, in Washington, my sisters had dragged me along to a local radio station, WDGD, where they hoped to try out for a popular radio drama called *Death on Wheels*. It wasn't Shakespeare. Its plots revolved around grisly automobile accidents. Even so, my sisters got stage fright and flubbed their lines.

I've never had much trouble getting up in front of a crowd. I delivered some lines from *Death on Wheels*, and became an instant success. Before I knew it, I was reading from a script every Friday evening with a small troupe of radio actors who played out the melodrama on the air.

In hindsight, my most notable fellow actor was a smart young man who made his living in those days selling Carstairs whisky. (None of us were paid for our parts in the radio show.) He had the gift of gab and was a nice guy too. Ross Martin went on to become famous as Artemis Gordon, the sidekick in the TV show and later the movie *The Wild, Wild West*.

It was a small jump, years later, from radio to stage and screen. In 1965, I wrote the score for the movie *In This Sign*. It had been pitched to me by a studio executive who was a friend of my sister Helen and her husband, Nick. The movie told the story of the Emperor Constantine, who adopted Christianity for the declining Roman Empire. He saw a cross in the clouds, and heard a voice that said, "In this sign, you shall conquer." The movie was a big Roman spectacle with plenty of battles and an interesting script.

I went to New York, to the offices of Magna Corporation, part of 20th Century Fox, to speak to George Skouros, the head of Magna. He was the brother of Spiros Skouros, a Hollywood big shot. George was in charge of this movie, and like most people in or connected to Hollywood, he was foul mouthed and argumentative, with a gigantic ego. Every other word out of his mouth was an expletive.

I spent an entire day with George. He pointed to a piano and said, "Show me what you can do. How would you portray Constantine?"

I played some of my musical ideas for him.

"Good," he said. "You're in." He ordered an assistant to get a script for me.

I wrote like mad for a year—my first big mistake in working for the movies. Don't believe anything anyone in Hollywood tells you. I wrote and wrote and wrote. I went back to see Skouros in New York. He seemed happy with what I'd done. "Keep up the good work," he said.

I should have asked for an advance or a retainer. Like a fool, I didn't. I gave Skouros a lot of my time and ideas. Fortunately, I never gave him my score. The final result was that the film was never made.

My second and last fling with Hollywood was almost as disappointing. I was hired to write the music for *The Group*, the movie based on Mary McCarthy's novel about a group of friends at Vassar College. Another musician was assigned to work with me. He told me the music would be all vocal—nothing orchestral. I wrote the strangest stuff. A lot of it was based on arrangements of music by one of Britain's greatest composers, Henry Purcell. The film's makers were going to have me conduct the music for the soundtrack. But the other guy beat me to it.

After I finished, I waited for my payment for a long time. When I called the producer, he said, "Oh, we thought you'd hang on. This is expected to go far and make a lot of money. That way, you'll get more than you bargained for." About six months went by, with no check.

I am a member of a very powerful musicians' union, and I went to see my representative in Washington. I got the check a few days later. It wasn't much. But at least it was what they'd promised.

It was hard work putting the music together. When I wrote music criticism for the *Washington Post,* I had to produce so many column inches of copy to make my stories fit in the allotted space. Writing for the movie was similar. I'd have to watch copies of the rushes with a stopwatch. The director would say, "I want 22 seconds here," and I'd have to fill the space.

They used my score, and the movie was made, but they credited just the name of my co-composer, Charles Gross, without mine, at my request. I didn't like the film.

My experience with the live stage in Washington was much better. From 1966 to 1968, I worked at the Arena Stage, using what little spare time I had to conduct the music for three plays: *Oh What a Lovely War,* Joan Littlewood's satire about war; *The Lonesome Train,* about Lincoln's funeral procession from Washington to Illinois; and *Hard Traveling,* set during the Great Depression.

Zelda Fichandler and her husband, Tom, had founded the beautifully designed theater in Southwest Washington, not far from the Potomac. It was a highly professional theater—the best in Washington, in fact. Zelda Fichandler had a talent for raking in contributions. She got millions from organizations like the Ford Foundation and the MacArthur Foundation. The place now houses four theaters, including the Round, where I conducted and rehearsed my players.

I worked with well-known artists like Ned Beatty, Ronnie Cox, Jane Alexander, Moses Gunn, the marvelous black actor, and Robert Foxworth, who was married to Elizabeth Montgomery. She later became famous as the benevolent witch in the TV show *Bewitched.*

Our actors did everything. I didn't know how I was going to get these actors to sing and dance. But they did it. Broadway used to have separate singers, dancers, and actors. No more. Due to budget constraints, the modern star has to combine all three talents. We helped start that trend in Washington. We had a drummer to keep the beat, and I rehearsed the songs over and over with the cast, playing my piano until they mastered the singing and dancing. These actors' minds were in the right place. They worked hard, and they had no problem. I taught them by rote, like a mother bird chirping and pitching food down her shrieking baby birds' throats.

I had established a reputation in Washington by then, and the Fichandlers called me and asked me to help. I had a lot of fun, though it meant plenty of long rehearsals starting in the mornings and stretching out through many evenings. It was at the Arena Stage that I learned how hard actors work. We'd rehearse each play for six weeks. And even though the actors worked hard, there was time enough for a lot of eye scratching, especially among the lady actors.

I loved to work in the theater, and to perform the down-to-earth popular music in the plays. It was a nice change from the rarified air of my normal classical routine. The music in each play was different. Ronnie Cox played his guitar in *Hard Traveling*. I got Benji Aranoff, the son of a friend of mine, to play banjo. He turned out to be one of the best banjo players in the country. Perhaps that shouldn't have surprised me. His father, Max, was a violist who had started the Curtis Quartet in Philadelphia.

I loved the theater, but with all my other roles in life—as pianist, conductor, teacher, composer, and administrator—I had to give up the stage after a couple of years. I just didn't have the time. It was good that I quit when I did, because soon I would take on the two most demanding jobs of my life.

8

Bach in Ireland

Chopin was the one for Truman. For me, it was Bach. Bach's *Mass in B Minor* is, to me, the Mount Everest of music—dignified, rare, disturbing yet consoling, and, like all great art, bigger than our mere human selves. I'd hoped to take over the Bethlehem Bach Festival after my mentor Ifor Jones resigned, in 1966. That didn't work out. A few years later, however, in 1970, my chance came in a small town in southwest Ireland, through a series of unlikely and strange events. Thus began ten very busy and stormy years that combined the music of Bach and the unlikely locale of Ireland.

Mary Brock, a journalist and close friend who'd worked for a small newspaper in Arlington, Virginia, had moved to Dublin and set up a business there. In those days, people still wrote personal letters on a regular basis. One of hers to me included the cryptic comment: "Do you know what the Midheaven is in your horoscope?"

I didn't even know what a Midheaven was. I wrote her back saying I hadn't the faintest idea.

She replied: "George, you have a Midheaven in three places on the globe, and one is right here in Killarney, Ireland. If you come to this town, you will be the golden boy."

I was skeptical, of course, and resisted her entreaties to come over, even though I liked to get out of Washington when I could. Usually I went to Greece for the summer, because I loved the place, spoke the language, and had a lot of friends there. But Mary Brock was persistent, and convinced me to at least stop in Ireland on my next trip to Greece.

I made the trip, stayed with Mary Brock in Dublin for a few days, and then obligingly took the train down to Killarney, where my supposed Midheaven lay, with absolutely no idea of what might be in store for me. The British Isles can have miserable weather, even in summer. It was rainy and cold when I got to Killarney. My thoughts ran to a warm sun beating down on a pleasant beach or restaurant in Greece. I called Mary Brock from my hotel in Killarney and told her that I wanted to leave town as soon as possible.

"All it does is rain down here, and there's no heat in these rooms, and I'm freezing to death," I reported.

"Have you been out walking?" she asked.

"No."

"Get out," she said. "Don't stay in your hotel room. Get out and walk."

I bought an umbrella and did as she commanded. There didn't seem to be much in Killarney. Two streets bordered by little shops formed a T. In the distance I could see an interesting cathedral. The surrounding countryside was said to be beautiful, although it was difficult to make out in the gloom and rain.

I love architecture, so I decided to take a closer look at the cathedral and its lovely spires that I'd made out from afar. Walking down the street, I noticed a shop window crowded with Waterford and Galway crystal. I decided to stop there on the way back because I'm a crystal freak.

The spires, it turned out, belonged to the Cathedral of St. Mary. And a very elegant and beautiful cathedral it was. This was the seat of the Bishop of Kerry, after all. In 1840, parishioners had commissioned the great English architect Augustus Welby Pugin to design the cathedral. But the Great Famine slowed construction, and the building wasn't completed until 1855, three years after Pugin had died.

The cathedral was especially beautiful because it sat in a field unoccupied by anything else except for a few cows. And the bishop's palatial residence next door. This, as the Irish said, was the bishop's throne and his palace.

After I inspected the cathedral inside and out, and from all sides, I walked back through the town and stopped in at the crystal shop I'd noticed earlier. Oddly, it had exactly the same address as Ifor Jones' old house in Bethlehem, Pennsylvania: 48 New Street.

Inside the shop, I picked out one of those beautiful, thick, woolen Irish sweaters to protect me from the wet and cold. When you wear them in the rain, the water runs off them. They last forever and they're warm as hell.

I got to talking with the shopkeeper, and I noticed immediately that she was very astute and inquisitive, which are typically Irish traits. The Irish have a penchant for finding out your name, where you're from, whether you're married or single, if you have money, what your job is, and where you're going. They almost invariably are blessed with an incomparable gift of gab. Sometimes it seems as if everyone in the country has kissed the Blarney Stone. They're all writers; everyone has published a book, it seems. Even the taxi driver knows more about politics than you ever will.

After I'd outlined my life history to the shopkeeper, whose name was Ina O'Connor, she seemed impressed—particularly that I was a professor at Catholic University. Although I was Greek Orthodox, rather than Catholic, the mere fact that I was associated with an institution with a name like Catholic University carried a lot of weight in as Catholic a country as Ireland. So did my title of professor, in a nation that had great respect for higher learning.

Ina O'Connor told me that she was on a search committee of locals dedicated to expanding Killarney's cultural horizons. The place already drew plenty of tourists, attracted by its beautiful mountains and lakes. But the search committee was looking to give Killarney a dash of brains as well as beauty.

"Well, you have a beautiful cathedral," I said. "Why not start a Bach festival?" I'd wanted to lead such an effort ever since my work with the Bethlehem Bach Festival in Pennsylvania.

With one hand on my sleeve and the other on the phone, Ina O'Connor began calling her colleagues on the search committee, almost as if to say, "I've got one!" The next thing I knew, I was sitting in a hotel having tea with O'Connor and two or three of her friends as we excitedly talked about launching a Bach festival in little Killarney.

I stayed on in my chilly hotel room for about two or three days. Mary Brock's bizarre vision had come true. Drawing on my experience at the Bethlehem Bach Festival and with the several orchestras and choral societies I'd launched and directed in Washington, I wrote notes in longhand on a yellow legal pad. The notes served as a primer on how to start and run a Bach festival, which is no small undertaking. After locating four spots in Killarney where our new festival's events could be held, including the cathedral, I went back to Dublin to confer with my old friend Mary Brock.

It was clear that a small town like Killarney couldn't muster the musical talent to launch a significant regional Bach festival. Much more was needed.

Brock was very helpful. She knew lots of people in Dublin. She introduced me to important players at Radio Telefis Eireann (RTE), the BBC of Ireland. I met a couple of composers there, including a big shot, Gerard Victory, whose work I later conducted in the United States. I found a lot of orchestra players at RTE, which had its own concert orchestra. Soloists were another matter. But I was told there were a lot of them hanging around in Dublin.

My new friends and I were discussing our start-up needs over lunch at the Shelbourne Hotel across from St. Stephen's Green in Dublin. Marika Guinness, the wife of the brewery heir Desmond Guinness, happened to be sitting nearby. She was related in some way to Kaiser Wilhelm. She and her husband lived in an excellent castle and were wealthy and powerful.

We'd been talking about throwing an introductory party at a hotel and inviting Dublin's musicians as a way to find soloists for the new Bach festival. Marika Guinness overheard our conversation and introduced herself. "Don't use a hotel," she said. "The Irish don't like to go to parties in hotels." She kindly offered us the use of an 18th-century Georgian townhouse she owned on one of Dublin's squares. The building was being redone at the time, and vacant, she explained. We could invite everyone we wanted. All we had to do was supply the food and drink, and candles for the candelabra, as the house had no electricity.

We stocked up on good food and liquor, including two types of Irish whiskey, and the party drew a mob. It didn't break up until three in the morning. There were conductors, singers, pianists, violinists, you name it, happily gorging themselves at the buffet table and imbibing generous cocktails. Ireland was still a poor country. Besides, everyone enjoys a free bash.

Mary Brock lined up another crucial supporter: Father Tom Fehily. In Ireland, whether you're Catholic or not, you don't get anywhere without the support of the cloth. Father Fehily became our little start-up festival's godfather. He helped smooth things over with the Bishop of Kerry, whose cooperation we needed for use of St. Mary's Cathedral and to make the festival a success in Killarney. The bishop was following Father Fehily's orders to help us, of course, but he was also happy that I was benefiting Killarney and Ireland. All of our musicians were Irish, after all.

There were two or three bishops of Kerry during my ten-summer tenure in Killarney. The most memorable bishop was caught red-handed having an affair with his cook. This was too bad, because he and I got along fine. I got to know the bishop well, and would have dinner with him in his palace. Once he invited me to his getaway house at Inch, a scenic resort, where he carried on with his housekeeper-cook during more private times. One of his priests chauffeured me there in the bishop's beautiful limo.

Some of the people in Killarney knew that the housekeeper was really the bishop's girlfriend. The scandal broke after my departure, when she became pregnant, moved to the United States, and had a child. The Vatican didn't defrock the bishop, but sent him to the jungles of Brazil to do missionary work. I've heard that the good bishop later returned to Ireland.

Pretty soon, after a lot of wheedling, wheeling, and dealing, I'd assembled a full chorus and orchestra, with a complement of excellent soloists. One was John O'Conor, the brilliant Irish pianist, who's enjoying great success today.

In the meantime, I had met the chief critic of the *Irish Times*, Charles Acton, and his wife, Carol. They were enthusiastic from the start, and really helped get the word out. Besides providing extensive newspaper coverage, Acton also wrote a magazine story about the event.

The festival, which had its inaugural in July 1970, was a success from the beginning, and continued so over its ten years of existence. The RTE even made a television documentary about the festival in 1973 that later aired on American public television. Unfortunately, it was recorded monaurally. But it conveyed something of the beauty of the music and the countryside.

The Killarney Bach Festival became even more popular with time. Each year's festival opened with a big party at Muckross House, an enormous estate that had belonged to the Bourn Vincent family. (The American businessman Bill Vincent, who owned the beautiful house in San Francisco where the TV series *Dynasty* was shot, was born in Muckross House.) Muckross sits a few miles outside the town of Killarney, near a couple of beautiful lakes, Muckross Lake and Lough Leane. Built in 1843, the estate had been visited by Queen Victoria in 1861.

VIPs from England, Scotland, France, the rest of Europe, and the United States began to come. Titled people would arrive. We always had prime ministers, ambassadors, and noblemen at the festival. The church would dispatch assorted archbishops. There were copious hors d'oeuvres, and champagne flowed freely at the festival's events. Gentlemen wore tuxedoes and the ladies gowns.

Ina O'Connor, shopkeeper and chairman of the festival, was in her ultimate glory. Soon Rolls-Royces and other luxury cars would pull up to her little shop on her little street in tiny downtown Killarney. Important people—"the swells," the Irish called them—would disembark from these luxury vehicles and go into O'Connor's store to pay homage to the great impresario, which she longed to be known as.

She lived above her shop in a little apartment. Originally, when you walked up a flight of stairs, you'd come into her master bedroom with a sink in the corner. To entertain all the new visitors, O'Connor had turned her bedroom into a proper sitting room. She had the sink removed and the room repapered and painted almost overnight. She served her guests the best bourbon and scotch and wine in the best crystal. The constant parade of important visitors made all the other shopkeepers on her street wildly envious, of course. But Ina O'Connor had finally achieved her lifelong dream of fame, and she relished every moment.

Her ego ballooned. She'd sit in an overstuffed easy chair in her converted sitting room like a queen holding court. Next to her was a bust of Bach, which I'd given her. Nearby, a portrait of me, and a baton. I've always conducted with my hands. I'd never used batons, but I'd brought a few along to Ireland. At times she'd hold my picture and my baton like Queen Elizabeth with her orb and scepter.

Although the Killarney Bach Festival was a success, it was expensive and time consuming for me to manage—especially given that I was in the United States for most of the year working at other jobs. And I wasn't being paid for the pain and pleasure of running the festival. My long-distance telephone bills ran to $500 or $600 a month as I tried to untangle the inevitable mare's nests that developed across the ocean.

The festival's board, unfortunately, was made up of small-town provincials who knew little or nothing about music, or about what was needed to bring off a major music festival. They'd start fires and I'd have to put them out.

Although the festival opened in July in its early years, I'd have to travel to Ireland in May to set things up. O'Connor and her crew were enthusiastic about the project, but had trouble following through on the many details that had to be attended to. Even simple things like concert programs seemed to get stuck in some strange Irish limbo. When I asked O'Connor who our printer would be, she replied, "Well, Jarge, I have a cousin in Cark"—she pronounced her o's like a's, in her Irish brogue—and then continued with a long-winded and complicated explanation of her fruitless struggle to find a printer.

I'd have to interrupt and say to her, "Ina, stop. You're going off into the wild blue yonder. This is all *myrianthopoulos*." That stopped her cold. Myrianthopoulos was not actually a Greek common noun. Rather, it was the surname of a good friend of mine in Washington, the talented geneticist and poet Ntino Myrianthopoulos. But Ina O'Connor didn't know that. I knew she wouldn't. I used it just to mean gobbledygook. In fact, she took to using the neologism herself, perhaps to impress her friends with her command of Greek.

"I asked you a question," I'd continue. "Can you answer that question?"

It turned out that there was no printer. So I had to get one. And the Killarney Town Hall hadn't yet been rented for our performance, so I had to take care of that. Plus a million other details. This is how it is if you live in Ireland. It is a lesson in insanity. Or, as George Bernard Shaw described the Emerald Isle upon his departure to England: "an autonomous political lunatic asylum."

Ina O'Connor had her strong points. She raised money like mad, with "that fatal Irish charm," as the Irish liked to call it. But she, the committee, and the Irish in general were driving me mad with their lack of organization and follow-through. In addition to pulling together the entire festival's music performance, I was forced to handle literally all of its many administrative tasks that were being ignored or simply mishandled. It was an impossibly full plate for me.

There were other depressing sidelights in Killarney. One of the famous music critics from London approached me and intimated that if my organization were to pay his airfare from England to Ireland, put him up in a hotel, and wine and dine him, he'd be very happy to write a nice review. For a brief moment, I thought back to Paul Hume's brave criticism of Margaret Truman's mediocre singing performance back in Washington. I told the English critic, in my nicest way, to jump in a lake. But journalists selling out is a more common practice than it should be, even in the United States.

Finally, ten years of the Killarney festival proved to be enough. I loved performing Bach, especially scaling the heights of his *B-minor Mass* every summer. The festival was a huge success. But dealing with the Irish in Killarney just became too much. They have the gift of gab. They can talk you right back into the lake and sink you. The members of my committee had meetings like mad. But they didn't know what they were doing.

When I left Ireland, I fell on my knees and said, "Thank God." I was so happy to leave that place. It's a beautiful country. The people are wonderful. The hospitality is unending. But don't try to do business there. It will drive you to drink, or to depart. Despite it all, the Killarney Bach Festival was a classic legacy for Ireland and for me.

9

A Gallery of Music

My music continued to take me to other countries, but not for such long stretches as Ireland. I played in Greece and Denmark. I was invited to Brazil, where I conducted in São Paulo and the new capital of Brasilia, carved out of the jungle in the country's vast interior.

Years earlier in Washington, it had been common for many of the musicians I worked with to take second or even third jobs as waiters or waitresses or in sales to make ends meet. That gradually ended with increasing prosperity in the United States and more powerful unions.

Brazil took me back to those early days in Washington, however. The musicians there were making $200 a month. After my second concert there, I refused payment. It wasn't that I'd become rich in my own career in music in the United States. I just felt guilty taking money when the musicians in my Brazilian orchestra were hardly scraping by.

But it was back in Washington, my home town, where I reached the pinnacle of my own career. In 1985, Richard Bales, who'd been music director at the National Gallery of Art for 42 years, decided to retire because of ill health. I was well known as a pianist and conductor in Washington by then. I'd played as a soloist and accompanist at numerous places in the city, including the National Gallery. The Gallery's director, J. Carter Brown, was an avid singer who'd been a member of one of my choral societies, the National Oratorio Society. Back at Harvard, Brown had been president of the glee club.

One day Brown called me up and asked me if I'd be interested in taking over as musical director at the National Gallery. Naturally I would, I said. The next day, we had a long chat in his office. I had to jump through a few more hoops. The hardest feat was to be accepted by a board of super-rich trustees who knew little or nothing about music. After nearly 50 years in classical music, however, I was more than aware of how to handle such folk. Soon I became the third—and last—musical director and conductor at the National Gallery.

The National Gallery got its start in 1941 with an extensive collection of art and a handsome bequest of money from Andrew W. Mellon, a former secretary of the U.S. Treasury and a member of the prominent and wealthy steel family in Pittsburgh. Beyond its art component, the National Gallery also had a music side. The National Gallery's first director, David Finley, had gone to England during World War II and had been tremendously impressed with the courage of Dame Myra Hess.

Many priceless national art treasures had been buried in Welsh coal mines or shipped to the United States to escape destruction by German bombs and by—who knew then?—perhaps worse. Living artistic treasures also left England and Europe to come to the safety of America's shores. Brilliant composers like Benjamin Britten and Sir Thomas Beecham were just a couple of examples.

But Dame Myra Hess, an amazing talent as a pianist, stayed on, helping to bolster British morale. When Finley got back to the United States, he told my predecessor, Richard Bales, that they had to do something similar at the new National Gallery, to help sustain American spirits during difficult times.

They started small, with a chamber orchestra, and gave weekly recitals in the National Gallery's garden court. Finley, his wife, and a few friends would scour the streets near the National Gallery and invite people, especially servicemen, to come in and listen to the music. To sweeten the pot, they threw in a free dinner with the music. Performances at the National Gallery were free, and they remain so today.

The musical aspect of the National Gallery got bigger and bigger, and the concerts became more frequent. When I got there in the 1980s, I had an orchestra of about 65 members. Occasionally I'd perform a concert that included a work by Mahler, which could require 80 players. We offered concerts and recitals, without fail, every Sunday at the Gallery at 7 p.m., October through June. And we packed the place every week. Long lines began to form Sunday afternoons for the 500 or 600 seats that would be available for each performance. We played in an unconventional setting: in the East or West Garden Court of the National Gallery. These spaces included lots of potted plants and trees, central fountains, celestially high ceilings, and beautiful columns, all of which lent the performances a unique classical air.

In my 18 years as music director at the National Gallery, I conducted more than 200 concerts: all the classical standards, plus some newer music. I've never sweated so much in my life. I worked that hard. With concerts or recitals every week, my musicians and I had little time for rehearsals. I fell back on a key piece of conducting and rehearsing advice from my old mentor at the Peabody Conservatory, Ifor Jones. Don't do what a lot of conductors do, he'd told me. Don't go into a historical monologue about what the composer of the piece happened to be doing or may have been thinking when he wrote the music. Just shut up and say, "Ladies and gentlemen, here's the tempo." And, off you go. Boom! Yell out orders as you go, or stop if you really need to explain something. But only give orders that will help the performers. Otherwise, don't talk.

Sometimes, we themed performances to mirror exhibitions. During the Goya Exhibition at the National Gallery, for example, we offered the first performance in Washington of the Italian composer Gian-Carlo Menotti's *Violin Concerto*. He was celebrating his 70th birthday, and his opera *Goya* was premiering at the Kennedy Center to our west on the Potomac River.

At the Gallery's American Music Festival, the longest-running festival of its kind, we featured jazz, which I love. Guest artists like George Shearing, Dizzie Gillespie, the Herbie Mann Trio, and the Billie Taylor Trio came to the National Gallery and played to full houses.

When Prince Charles and Princess Diana came to town, there was a lot of hoopla, of course. The National Gallery's administration put me and my orchestra up in one of the balconies of the Gallery's enormous new building. We played entrance music as the royal couple glided down a grand staircase. It was a recessional by the British composer Sir Edward Elgar—the same one that had been played at Charles and Diana's wedding. They had come to see the exhibition *Treasure Houses of Great Britain*, and had snuck up in an elevator in private so they could make their grand public descent down the stairway. Things were much more formal, I decided, than when President Truman had entertained the future Queen Elizabeth and her consort Philip at Blair-Lee House so many years before. But we had entered the Reagan era in America, and there was much more pomp everywhere. People were dressed very formally.

If you were to ask me to name my favorite concert of the many that we performed at the National Gallery, it would be hard to say. I liked them all. And I felt blessed to be conducting them. I'm not a Catholic, but I used to cross myself before going onstage at every performance. Where else could I get an opportunity like this—to conduct what I pleased, and how I pleased? I'd conducted before, but the performances at the National Gallery were the highlight of my career—along with brief interludes of peace in a sea of troubles in Killarney. Because I often said to the Good Lord that if He'd permit me to conduct Bach's *B-minor Mass*, He could take me in. I was fortunate to have the joy of doing that every year at the National Gallery and in Killarney.

Of course, the National Gallery was a federal project, authorized by Congress, and it was not without its hassles. Chief among these was Washington's stifling bureaucracy. I got a taste of this as soon as I started. I couldn't get my own parking space for my car, which I drove into the city from my home in Bethesda every day. Instead, I had to run outside from my office every couple of hours to feed a parking meter.

When I told Carter Brown about the problem, he seemed imperturbed. When I threatened to quit, he said, "Oh, I'm sorry to hear that. We'll miss you." Finally, he relented, and got me my own parking space.

But bigger problems were in the offing. Union wages skyrocketed for musicians during my tenure. A concert that cost $7,500 in 1985 when I started would have run $35,000 during my last year at the National Gallery in 2003. The cost of labor began to set limits on how big an orchestra I could field.

Then I began to become a kind of ambassador for the National Gallery by default. This was not something I was particularly interested in or suited to doing. I was a professional musician. And I had plenty of other things to do already in my capacity as musical director.

Nevertheless, I often found myself playing goodwill ambassador. Seldom did anyone give me notice of who was coming. One day Queen Sonja of Sweden showed up at the National Gallery. Much to my surprise, I had to represent the institution to her, although others would have been far better qualified for the job.

Likewise with Stephen Sondheim, the Broadway composer, and also with a woman who identified herself as Puccini's granddaughter. When these people appeared at my door, I called the department of external affairs. "Do the best you can," they said. And I did. But it didn't strike me as a professional way to run such a large and respected institution.

The final straw for me came when the design department began encroaching on my musical turf during my rehearsals in the National Gallery's garden courts. Employees from the design department would wander in as we practiced. Then tourists began milling about. Of course, it became difficult for the players to concentrate—which I'd let the interlopers know in a very loud voice, if a sullen glare didn't succeed in shooing them away.

But the sad fact is that the whole National Gallery was run by a bureaucratic administrator who didn't give a hoot or a holler about the music or the art on the walls. He was there to run the place like a government agency. And the bureaucrats drove me crazy. I never hated anyone as much as I hated those people. I hated the people in Killarney because of their stupidity. But they had an excuse.

They were inexperienced. They were provincials. People at the National Gallery had a lot more education and knowledge of the world. But many of them seemed to work at making the place a depressing, stolid, uncomprehending bureaucracy. I resigned in 2003.

My life has been placid ever since. I've continued to work on some compositions, including Greek songs based on poetry by my late good friend Ntino Myrianthopoulos. He'd worked at the National Institutes of Health until he died, and had always been my main source of poetry for my Greek songs.

I continue to live in my longtime home in Bethesda during the warmer months. Seeking escape from Maryland's bitter winters, I began to visit Palm Beach, Florida, during high season about ten years ago at the suggestion of a good friend there. I almost bought an apartment there, but it was sold out from under me during the speculative real estate frenzy in Florida.

In Palm Beach, I met Agnes Ash, a fascinating woman who, with her husband, wrote and edited the *Palm Beach Daily News*, better known as the *Shiny Sheet*, a society newspaper, and a magazine called *Palm Beach Life*. (The *Shiny Sheet* was so called because it was printed on slick paper, so that the ink would not rub off and soil its privileged readers' hands.) Aggie Ash went around town with a five-and-dime notebook and a pen in hand. As such, she was invited to every party in town offered by every society matron.

We'd sit and have lunch in nice places in Palm Beach like Toojay's and Charley's Crab, and be constantly interrupted by women inviting Ash to their fetes. It seemed to be their foremost desire in life to get into the pages of one of Ash's publications.

None of this intense social striving seemed to affect Ash, who was very down to earth and had both feet on the ground. She had a wonderful personality. Ash had my friend Garnett Stackelberg of Washington cover Palm Beach society, which was a brilliant move. She was known as Baroness Stackelberg because she was married to the Estonian Baron Constantine Steno von Stackelberg, a cousin of Lord Mountbatten and a relative of European royalty. In Palm Beach, royalty reigns. Baroness Stackelberg made huge waves, even though she was born in Nebraska. She used to tell me that folks in Palm Beach would curtsy to her. They didn't know that you don't have to curtsy to a baroness.

Not all was as it seemed in Palm Beach, Ash told me. Behind those imposing hedges and beyond those expansive lawns, some people were subsisting off Campbell's Soup or canned tuna fish in order to save enough money to keep up outward appearances. Because money, new or old, never lasts.

I once met a countess in Killarney who introduced me to her nephew. She had a home in Palm Beach, she told me. Later on, when I told Aggie Ash about her, Ash explained to me that the young man wasn't the countess's nephew. He was what Palm Beach society called a walker—someone who escorted wealthy, older women to social events. He lived with her and decorated her house, Ash said. But the couple had come to a bad end. They just disappeared one day. I asked Ash what had gone wrong. Nothing really, she said. The money just ran out and they had to sell the house.

Friends of mine from Washington had winter refuges on Sanibel Island and in Naples, on the Gulf Coast of Florida about 100 miles west of Palm Beach. I went over and looked at Florida's west coast, after I lost out on the apartment I'd hoped to buy in Palm Beach. I liked the quiet atmosphere in Naples. (It has grown a lot less quiet in the decade since as traffic and construction have hit nearly cancerous levels.) I bought an apartment in Naples.

Then, I decided that I wanted to play piano in Florida as well as in Maryland. So I bought a house, where I could pound away without disturbing the neighbors. Here I happily remain in the winter, playing when I can, and enjoying the warm weather. In the summer, I return to my old home in Bethesda. Health problems have kept my conducting to a minimum since I left the National Gallery in Washington.

I did return to the Gallery in June 2007, however, to guest-conduct the National Gallery Orchestra for a night of Mendelssohn, Beethoven, and Brahms. As usual, the place was packed, and the audience enthusiastic. I could not stand for the whole performance, so I conducted while sitting. Even so, I was sore afterward for a day or two from the physical exertion of waving my arms and moving my head while conducting. Nevertheless, it was good to be back, and the orchestra played magnificently.

Epilogue

In looking back, all of my musical life and career seem to fuse together. Beginning as a so-called musical prodigy; moving on in my late teens to become a Marine sergeant and the personal presidential pianist to President Harry Truman for four years of person-to-person history. Then my music took me to the podiums and stages of Washington and other places, nationally and internationally, in what now seems the blink of an eye. Finally came my 18 years as musical director and conductor of the National Gallery Symphony. It has been, for me, a most wonderful life in music.

I've spent most of that life in a very political city. The lives and careers of politicians and musicians are very different. For a time, Truman's life and mine intersected. Of course, I was too young then to understand many of the complicated political issues that Truman and his men were dealing with. But I grew to respect and love the man. There was no pretense or false pride in him. Working with him was like working with one of my father's close friends—like being with a wonderful, friendly gentleman who was a loving father and husband.

Truman's demeanor never changed during the years that I knew him. The presidency and politics simply were his job. And he did that job very well, as he had done with all his previous work. He was an effective leader partly because he made himself so easily understood. He was direct and he took a real interest in those around him. People responded to those genuine qualities, and many were devoted to him. I never got the impression, as I have with many politicians and people in other walks of life, that behind his personality lurked a political opportunist preoccupied with his own self-importance. I can only hope that I did my job with something approaching his intelligence, thoroughness, modesty, honesty, and perseverance.

If politics were the art of the possible for him—what could be accomplished in a sometimes selfish, often confusing, always changing real world—music was the art of the impossible—a higher plane, an idealized state of consciousness. I was fortunate that my own talents allowed me to bring him, and many others, to that elevated level, if only for a short time. I can only hope that many more in the future will derive the solace and satisfaction from music that Truman and I were so lucky to enjoy.

Music has been for me, much as it was for Harry Truman, a beautiful representation of the world as it ought to be, rather than it is. A chance to soar above the mundane and walk with the immortals, if only for a few brief moments. I've been fortunate indeed to make a living and a life out of music.

I think that Truman might agree that only by persevering through the difficulties and adversities of everyday life can we hope to rise occasionally to the heights where great music and art can bring us. Conceived and played by humans, music too is very much the art of the possible.

Each of us served that art to the best of his ability. I come back to my mentor Truman's words: "Whatever happened, throughout, I did the best I could."

Index

Note: page numbers followed by an "f" refer to figures or photographs.

978-0-595-48716-5
0-595-48716-5